MARCO TOSA

Barbie®

FOUR DECADES OF FASHION, FANTASY, AND FUN

Harry N. Abrams, Inc., Publishers

Translated from the Italian by Linda M. Eklund
Editor, English-language edition: Amy L. Vinchesi
Design coordinators, English-language edition:
Tina Thompson, Ellen Nygaard Ford

**Library of Congress Cataloging-in-
Publication Data**
Tosa, Marco, 1955–
    [Mille volti di un mito.   English]
    Barbie : four decades of fashion, fantasy,
and fun / Marco Tosa ; translated from the
Italian by Linda M. Eklund.
        p.   cm.
    Includes bibliographical references and
index.
    ISBN 0–8109–4008–6 (hardcover)
    1. Barbie dolls.   I. Title.
NK4894.3.B37T6713   1998
688.7'221'0973—dc21   98–22776

Printed and bound in Spain

688.7221

Harry N. Abrams, Inc.
100 Fifth Avenue
New York, N.Y. 10011
www.abramsbooks.com

Contents

page 7   Barbie from Doll to Icon: A Few Reflections

page 19   A Short Walk Through History: Tradition and Change

page 47   Barbie and Haute Couture: 1959

page 77   Barbie and Fashion: From 1960 On

page 113   Barbie in the Mirror: Professions and Pomp

page 135   Barbie and the Colors of the World: A Cross-Cultural Journey

page 148   Barbie Approaches the Millennium

page 150   Index of Models

page 152   Selected Bibliography

Barbie

A Few Reflections

from Doll to Icon

To make a prairie it takes a clover

and one bee, —

One clover, and a bee,

And revery.

The revery alone will do

If bees are few.

(Emily Dickinson, *The Collected Poems of Emily Dickinson*)

Facing page:
John Baldessari,
Kiss Kiss.

This page: Barbara
Nessim, ***Imelda***
Marcos Ain't Got
Nothing on Me.

Barbie Millicent Roberts; sign of Leo; daughter of Robert and Margareth Roberts. Probably only a few people know that Barbie, the most famous doll in the world, has a first and last name, parents, and a way to consult her horoscope. In the real world such humanistic identification can be perplexing, since we habitually view toys as simple consumer products. To invest a doll with such realistic attributes, however, makes the game a little more interesting. It imbues her with a credibility that, as we shall see, is the most significant aspect of this woman in miniature, and the driving force behind her success. The fact that she is an "adult," at 11½ inches tall has allowed, and continues to allow, a multitude of little girls and adolescents access to the forbidden world of grownups, imitating their habits and attitudes courtesy of the imaginative metamorphosis that occurs in children's play.

Robert A. M. Stern,
Colossus of Barbie.
*A cultural legacy of
ancient Egypt lives
again in this monu-
mental reinterpretation
of the most famous
doll in the world,
executed in gesso,
sand, and wood.
Photo by Jessica
Katz.*

*Facing page: Kenny
Scharf,* **Barbluella**,
*acrylic on canvas.
An unparalleled
model, Barbie
suggests endless
possibilities to artists.
The portrait, in this
case, is undeniably
the most fascinating,
with its kaleidoscope of
techniques and styles.*

This adult universe of glamorous appearances is recreated around Barbie, who is sheltered from and unspoiled by the stresses and ambitious drives that torment "real adults," for whom appearances often become the oppressive burden of everyday life. One enters the fantastic world of Barbie for a few years with a single objective—to play at being grown up, maybe even mocking adults a little by accentuating their vices and manias but, above all, feeling closer to them, more like them, less isolated within a childhood that may be full of solitude. Some kids are parked in front of the television at an early age, staring with wondering eyes, mesmerized for hours, well-behaved and mute, letting their busy parents relax a little. As a result, the ability to make choices and form individual opinions may be compromised, while their expectations of the future are modeled on 30-second commercial spots. When they find time to play and to free their imaginations, the comfort and complicity of their toys are a welcome reprieve from the land of TV and solitude.

A Doll Like Any Other?

From the dawn of time, dolls have been the silent allies of children at play, adapting themselves to social patterns and accepting the demands imposed by their little owners. Passive and docile, the dolls are simultaneously exalted and condemned, the target of the adult world's sweeping passions that range from unmitigated hatred to the most tender love.

Our Barbie doll, who has been subjected to media criticism, feminist and intellectual fault-finding, and the accusations of pedagogues, has nonetheless inherited the same duties as her antecedents, and she joins them in performing their traditional functions in the world of make-believe.

Times have certainly changed and Barbie, in a manner quite different from other toys, has adapted quickly to an ever-evolving market in order to stay competitive and continue building her widespread commercial success. Can we blame her?

The figure of Barbie, for all its positive and negative interpretations, is larger than the sum of its parts. Her enormous popularity among children is the foundation of her success, casting her as a sort of colossus in miniature, resistant to outside aggression. We really ought to ask ourselves how such a simple toy, whose underlying concept is so similar to nineteenth-century dolls/mannequins, can provoke so much criticism and rage.

Perhaps to adults Barbie is the perfect scapegoat, a ubiquitous reminder of a way of life mirrored with discomforting realism.

We will return to these modest reflections during the effort to comprehend this sensational pop icon of the 1960s, the undisputed queen of the modern international toy market.

The Art of Barbie

The symbolism and evocative force behind this doll are bound inextricably to the memories of many generations of Barbie lovers, who do not judge her for disappointing their fantasies, but rather cling to the pleasant illusoriness of her trademark shocking pink world. Barbie's influence has transcended racial, geographic, and cultural confines to create a kind of mythology, one that has inspired a multitude of artists, painters, sculptors, photographers, etc. Using her as a model or a formal pretext for their work, they have created a distinctive artistic genre that can be readily defined as "The Art of Barbie," the title of a group show in New York City that brought many of these artists together in 1995. Whether best described as fine art or simply as a craft, their work is a point of pride for Mattel. As an object for public consumption, Barbie is vulnerable to every interpretation, which is the nature of having such a powerful identity.

The origins of Barbie are rooted in the creative process—the continual quest for new designs for body features and mechanisms, and the endless planning and production of her massive wardrobe in its precise replication of the "real world"—which partially explains and helps the consumer to fathom the Barbie phenomenon.

If we are to know Barbie and her universe, we have to touch on the "sacred" issues, i.e. the history, philosophy, pedagogy, and psychoanalysis surrounding her image. Because no toy has ever been so wedded to the day-to-dayness of real life and so widely distributed among so many different social contexts, the resulting conflicts of opinion—the tangle of "sacred vs. profane," if you will—is inevitable.

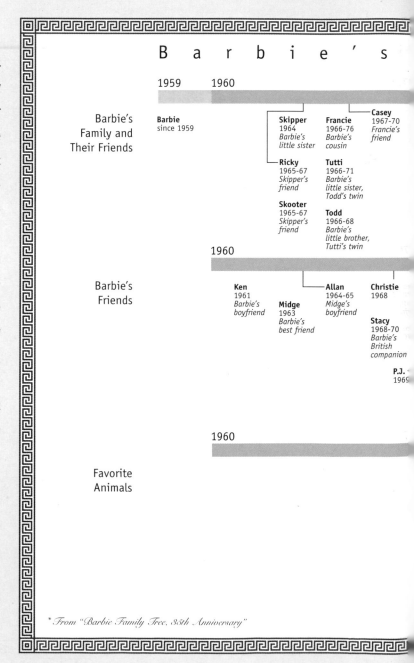

Barbie's

1959   1960

Barbie's Family and Their Friends

Barbie since 1959

Skipper 1964 *Barbie's little sister*

Francie 1966-76 *Barbie's cousin*

Casey 1967-70 *Francie's friend*

Ricky 1965-67 *Skipper's friend*

Tutti 1966-71 *Barbie's little sister, Todd's twin*

Skooter 1965-67 *Skipper's friend*

Todd 1966-68 *Barbie's little brother, Tutti's twin*

1960

Barbie's Friends

Ken 1961 *Barbie's boyfriend*

Midge 1963 *Barbie's best friend*

Allan 1964-65 *Midge's boyfriend*

Christie 1968

Stacy 1968-70 *Barbie's British companion*

P.J. 196⁹

1960

Favorite Animals

From "Barbie Family Tree, 35th Anniversary"

10
....

The "Message" of Barbie

And what might we observe about Barbie's "message" beyond the usual superficial musings, the commonplace reactions that dwell on empty consumerism and appearances? Certainly her cheery, pert demeanor can be annoying and lead one to suspect she is nothing more than a big empty dress at a party.

Barbie's family tree, required reading if you want to know and distinguish among the many members of her clan.

F a m i l y   T r e e *

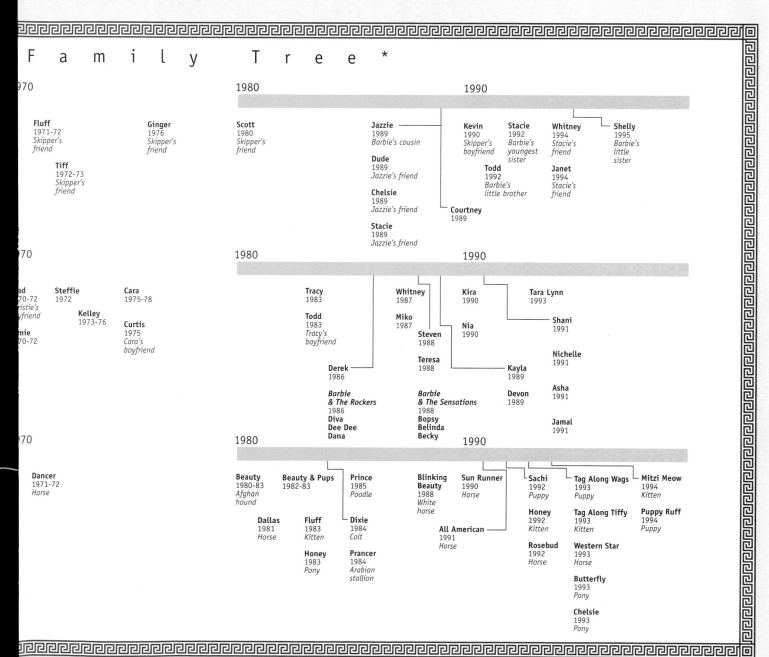

1970   **1980**   **1990**

Fluff
1971-72
Skipper's friend

Ginger
1976
Skipper's friend

Tiff
1972-73
Skipper's friend

Scott
1980
Skipper's friend

Jazzie
1989
Barbie's cousin

Dude
1989
Jazzie's friend

Chelsie
1989
Jazzie's friend

Stacie
1989
Jazzie's friend

Courtney
1989

Kevin
1990
Skipper's boyfriend

Todd
1992
Barbie's little brother

Stacie
1992
Barbie's youngest sister

Whitney
1994
Stacie's friend

Janet
1994
Stacie's friend

Shelly
1995
Barbie's little sister

1970   **1980**   **1990**

...ad
...0-72
...ristie's ...friend

Steffie
1972

Cara
1975-78

Kelley
1973-76

Curtis
1975
Cara's boyfriend

...mie
...0-72

Tracy
1983

Todd
1983
Tracy's boyfriend

Derek
1986

Barbie & The Rockers
1986
Diva
Dee Dee
Dana

Whitney
1987

Miko
1987

Steven
1988

Teresa
1988

Barbie & The Sensations
1988
Bopsy
Belinda
Becky

Kira
1990

Nia
1990

Kayla
1989

Devon
1989

Tara Lynn
1993

Shani
1991

Nichelle
1991

Asha
1991

Jamal
1991

1970   **1980**   **1990**

Dancer
1971-72
Horse

Beauty
1980-83
Afghan hound

Beauty & Pups
1982-83

Dallas
1981
Horse

Prince
1985
Poodle

Fluff
1983
Kitten

Honey
1983
Pony

Dixie
1984
Colt

Prancer
1984
Arabian stallion

Blinking Beauty
1988
White horse

All American
1991
Horse

Sun Runner
1990
Horse

Sachi
1992
Puppy

Honey
1992
Kitten

Rosebud
1992
Horse

Tag Along Wags
1993
Puppy

Tag Along Tiffy
1993
Kitten

Western Star
1993
Horse

Butterfly
1993
Pony

Chelsie
1993
Pony

Mitzi Meow
1994
Kitten

Puppy Ruff
1994
Puppy

removed from its original historical function—becomes the vehicle for sensitizing future generations to controversial debates.

How then to answer those who shun her fashionable wardrobe and lifestyle filled with the trappings of wealth and privilege as pretentious and over the top? This critique seems almost too easy, and is certainly not limited to Barbie. Besides, criticism is an inevitable product of consumerism, so it serves us better to salvage the good in this universe of permanent plastic smiles and formal evening dresses. The principal lesson to be gleaned is one of self-esteem, looking after oneself and others, and, beyond this, establishing bonds with friends and family, lessons that gradually move a child closer to the adult world in a tender, nonthreatening manner.

The Quest for Barbie

We are going to take an intentionally radical narrative route to dissect this unusual doll, free from conventional objectives and open to many individual theses. We will consider each hypothesis, explaining some more closely and bypassing others that have been debated to exhaustion. Indeed, compiling a detailed and truly in-depth survey of Mattel's enormous output of Barbie products and accessories would require an encyclopedic treatment, something that has already been done successfully by certain American scholars on the subject.

Given the exhaustive amount of books and publications aimed exclusively at Barbie collectors, it would be futile—overkill, even—to shape this analysis in the same vein. Instead, we will seek a better understanding and

Once we get beyond these facile observations, however, and analyze the evolution of Barbie and her ideology more carefully, a different reality emerges, one that is undoubtedly simplified yet remains positive. In it, our doll becomes the lead character in an enterprise that instructs children to care about nature, animals, and the environment in a language adapted for them. The simplicity of that language may be disputed, but it is direct and comprehensible. The promulgation of this very relevant and contemporary message is fundamentally important, especially when it is entrusted to a product with such great powers of dissemination. For the first time a toy—in a role

explanation of this doll's evolution by revealing its credible historical elements.

Fashion will intrinsically be the star of this story: powerful, evocative, the essence of Barbie and her world. She is its ideal interpreter, the indivisible unification of form and content. Beyond that, she is a precise point of reference for the tastes and trends that reigned in the 1960s, before the glory days of haute couture—the heyday of fashion design—ceased to be. For this reason, the larger focus will be devoted to describing Barbie's wardrobe from 1959, the year she appeared on the American market, up through the late 1970s, when the fickle, ever-evolving world of fashion became dominated by the giant international ready-to-wear labels, which radically altered the function and quality of many designs.

Barbie is many things to many people. A few notes on her technical and industrial evolution will serve to advance our knowledge of this singular doll, while observations about her representations of a mélange of social and cultural identities and on her remarkable capacity to assimilate new archetypes will help to overcome time-worn ideas.

We will take a light narrative path then, without a preconceived scheme, and arranged chiefly to arouse interest in the undeniable pleasures that this little doll engenders. We will not forget, however, that in the ongoing allegory of life continually staged by Barbie, the boundaries between truth and make-believe mirror the fine lines between one's own sense of reality and play.

Barbie

1. *Various phases in developing the model for Barbie's head.*

2. *Enlarged and reduced prototypes in resin epoxy.*

14
....

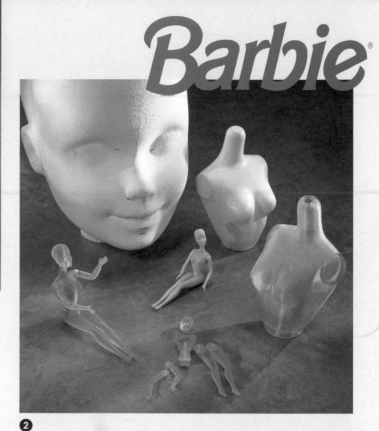

3. *Enlarged cast and busts of Barbie made of opaque and transparent resin.*

4–5. *"Master mold" in metal of the torso and a positive of the mold in wax.*

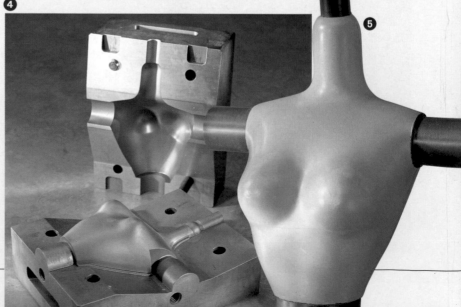

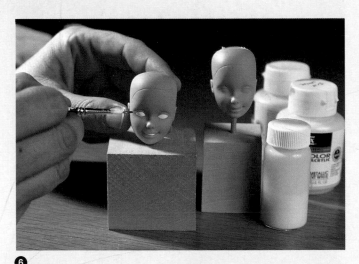

6

7

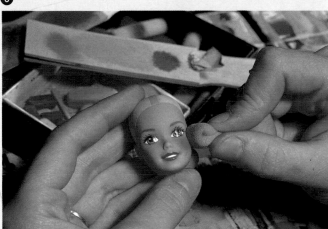

8

9

6–8. *Various phases in the manual decoration of the facial prototype. Delineation of the features and the application of makeup are carefully executed in sequential steps to achieve the desired design.*

9. *The finished face will serve as a reference model for future serial production.*

10. *A sample set of heads with different skin colorations. With the appropriate makeup, they will represent a great variety of races and body types.*

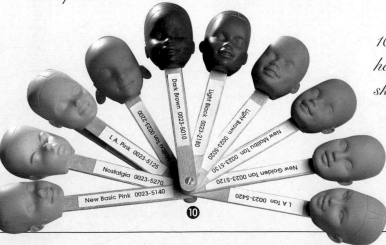

10

L.A. Pink 0023-5125

Nostalgia 0023-5270

New Basic Pink 0023-5140

Dark Brown 0023-5010

Light Black 0023-2180

Light Brown 0023-5020

New Malibu Tan 0023-5130

New Golden Tan 0023-5120

L.A. Tan 0023-5420

A Few Reflections

⑪

11–12. Display blocks support head prototypes ready for decoration. Using a basic model cut from a single die, different facial features can be achieved with subtle makeup applications.

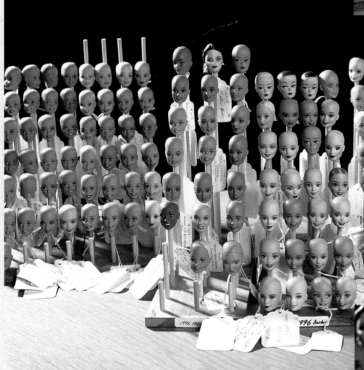

16

⑫

13. Final versions of the head molds—or "master heads"— establish production parameters for the manufacturers.

⑬

⑭

⑮

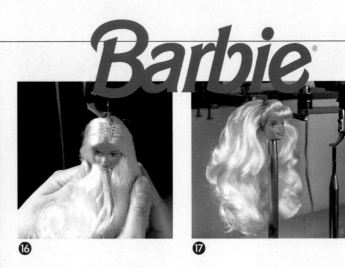
⑯

⑰

⑱

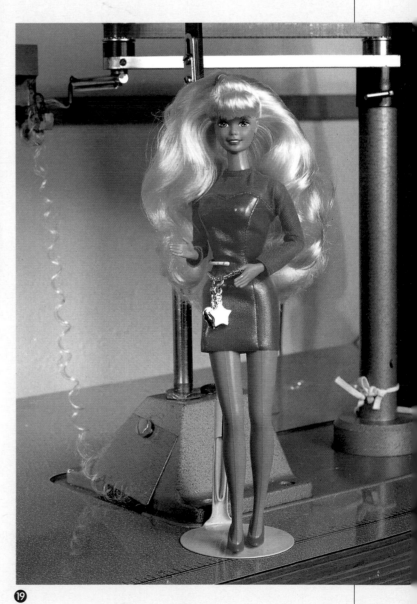
⑲

14–18. The finished vinyl head is then ready for the hair-styling division. The softness of the synthetic material allows a continuous strand of hair to be sewn directly into the head in a rotary pattern. The hair's part, bangs, or other details are made by hand in this phase.

19. The finished doll is ready for packaging.

A Short Walk

Through History

Tradition and Change

BASIC BARBIE DOLL FASHION MODEL SET

Your Barbie doll is created of sturdy flesh-tone vinyl plastic. Moveable arms, legs and head make it easy to dress Barbie in her exciting fashion model's wardrobe. Barbie Doll, plus striped jersey swimsuit, sun glasses, pearl earrings and shoes — and special pedestal to keep Barbie on her feet for all Fashion Shows. $3.00

Facing page: Barbie Number One (1959) with her original packaging.

Left: A sketch of the doll from the 1960 catalog.

19

I am Memory, and am wise in lore of the past, but I too am old. These beings were like the waters of the River Than, not to be understood. Their deeds I recall not, for they were but of the moment.

(H. P. Lovecraft, "Memory." Originally published in June, 1919 in "The United Co-operative")

During the second half of the nineteenth century, one of the most prestigious shops in Paris, Au Paradis des Enfants, specialized in the sale of the most sought-after and costly dolls produced by the French toy industry. To its young customers, the shop gave a tiny "Album de la Poupée," measuring 2¼ x 1½ inches, which served as both a catalog of dolls and the shop's business card. Along with the address and other advertising copy, the little book offered on each page a selection of photographs of beautiful dolls elegantly attired, from which the most fortunate girls could choose their favorite. This little catalog of fashion in miniature was both a valuable promotional tool and a young girl's first invitation to the female adult world.

Illustrations of these elegant ensembles date between 1867 and 1873, and are complete right down to their meticulous accessories. Each was photographed with studious attention to the pose and countenance of the dolls. These artifacts are only slightly more curious than some of the other material available today that documents the historical production and distribution of dolls and doll accessories. These catalogs are particularly significant when compared to the larger ones that would serve the same purpose more than a century later in advertising Barbie, the most famous doll in the world.

Barbie as Coming-of-Age Companion

As Barbie's growing popularity and success has skyrocketed in the last few years, so has the heavy criticism surrounding her image, the sources of which are endless. However, beneath the critical attitude is usually a scant knowledge of the actual history relating to the doll/object and to its changing role over the years.

The scholar Carla Rocchi published an essay entitled *I due volti standardizzati della bambola contemporanea* [*The Two Standardized Faces of the Contemporary Doll*] in Volume 16 of *La Rivista Folklorica* in 1987. She took a hypercritical stance in her analysis of the far-reaching Barbie phenomenon. "The huge success of this automaton, who is infinitely offensive and noneducational, must have some explanation other than the persuasive power of advertising. We have to ask ourselves why, instead of being a little girl, Barbie is explicitly an adult, with adult tastes, problems, and obligations."

Barbie is not the first doll to take the form of a grown woman; historically, those dolls that functioned as playthings—that could not, in other words, be confused with the amulets and fetishes of ancient cultures—also resembled and shared the anatomy of the adult female, with obvious sexual characteristics. One of the more notable examples is the doll found on May 10, 1889, when Roman excavations brought to light the sarcophagus of Crepereia Tryphaena. It contained a splendid ivory adult doll with related garb dated circa 150–160 A.D.

Official portraiture done over the centuries has presented evidence of the ownership of toys as an expression of status. Young royalty and noblewomen were painted with dolls that were always in the form of adult women. Among the many significant paintings in this regard are *Charity* by Lucas Cranach, from 1537, and Johann Zoffany's eighteenth-century portrait of the grandchildren of Maria Theresa of Austria.

The nineteenth century was a golden period for the establishment and dissemination of dolls. They had become an industrial and commercial phenomenon in countries like France and Germany, where an endless army of them was produced in all kinds of traditional materials, such as wood, wax, papier mâché, and porcelain. The dolls were produced in the image of the adult woman, as was very obviously illustrated by the pretty mannequins from the little Parisian catalog cited earlier.

The customary function of these dolls as harbingers of fashion trends slowly began to be replaced by the increased circulation of women's magazines dedicated to this same topic. It is partly as a result of this that the famous "poupées parisiennes," those symbols of refined elegance, began to target the juvenile market. Under Napoleon III, the new middle class began looking to expensive playthings to achieve a higher social recognition and identity for their children. It was not by chance that these dolls came furnished with the luxurious wardrobes exemplary of the social and moral precepts essential to the breeding of a real lady; they were educational and behavioral models for early training in adulthood. They were a reassuring image of femininity, as well as a mirror of the formal, restricted destiny of women of that period, much like the corsets worn by mothers, daughters, and dolls alike.

Barbie Number One (1959) with her familiar hairdo— the "Ponytail" with curly bangs—that accurately represents the style of that time. She is wearing the famous knit bathing suit in black-and-white stripes, gold metal hoop earrings, and the obligatory high heels. The holes under her feet, characteristic of the series commonly known today as Number One, correspond to holes in the soles of her shoes. The holes were reinforced with little brass rings and cylinders that fit onto studs in the plastic pedestal that was packaged with the doll.

21

The fixed appearance of those charming dolls with their pale, smiling porcelain heads was overcome by the continual changing of their clothes, at once a part of the game and a lesson. The dolls' ensembles for day and evening, for outdoor excursions, and for receiving guests reflected the superficial rituals of good manners. The relationship between dolls and fashion is undeniably tight, united in every epoch through consumerism reflective of the historical period. Dolls of every type, from babies to adults, have evolved throughout our social system without ever losing their basic focus: the need to be dressed, whether in a rich and up-to-date wardrobe or in simple rags stitched to their backs. The nude doll does not exist in our imagination; with no clothes she is incomplete, socially unprepared. One's first thought is always to cover her up, perhaps embarrassed by her nakedness.

The doll's role in the game of life is merely reflective of the society that produced her. A doll has no pretense of her own. She is not "born" autonomous and whole. She is our puppet, passive, accepting, content to be shaped and molded in our hands as we imitate gods in the rites of creation. Thus, we really cannot accuse a doll of being "non-educational;" she is the product of the same culture of which she is a mirror, along with countless other toys and games of questionable educational merit.

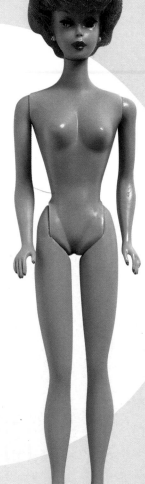

Crepereia Tryphaena, a Roman ivory doll dating from 150– 160 A.D., and a "Bubble Cut" Barbie from 1961. The similarities of form are immediately evident, imbuing a timeless quality.

Putting aside these complex issues for a moment, the fact remains that these dolls are wanted and loved, preserved with loving care, and bound to us as mute witnesses to a culture that is based on appearances. A faithful reference to and fount of information for the study of fashion history, the army of dolls from the past—especially those from the 1800s—constitutes the best foundation

Above: **Charity**, detail of the 1537 painting by Lucas Cranach. Once again, the doll depicted represents an adult woman.

Above left: Cornelis Troost, **Family Group in a Room** (detail), 1739.

Below: Cut-out paper dolls from a folio published circa 1870–75 and watercolored by hand. The adult woman is always the lead character in a young girl's world of play.

Agnes.

Martha.

Tradition and Change

*"Bild Lilli," a doll produced in Germany in 1955 by the Hausser Elastolin firm in Neustad. Designed by Max Weissbrodt and manufactured in rigid plastic, the doll measures 11½ inches tall and is modeled on the eponymous character from the comic strip drawn by Reinhard Beuthien that appeared after 1952 in the newspaper **Bild Zeitung**. The Lilli doll is the model on which the Barbie doll is based; as the smaller photo at right shows, the conceptual and aesthetic analogies between Lilli and Barbie are undeniable.*

for understanding the doll that would become Barbie, who is not so different, after all, from those whom she would follow.

1945: The Birth of Mattel

The story of Barbie, or rather, the sequence of events and coincidences that led to her creation, began in 1938 when a young couple, Elliot and Ruth Handler, arrived in Los Angeles. Various personal and professional ups and downs engaged the couple, leading finally in 1945 to the birth of

the toy company named "Mattel," now a famous trademark, in which "Matt" stands for Mattson and "El" for Elliot. Old friends Harold Mattson and Elliot Handler worked together in a garage they had converted into a small creative studio, planning, designing, and producing handmade wood products—first painted picture frames and, later, furniture and fixtures for dollhouses. Ruth, who was already the mother of two young children, had innate and formidable commercial instincts. As a collaborator in her husband's work, she used her suggestions and ideas to shift the new company toward a product line with more toys. Along with the doll furniture, they began

Lilli

Lilli: bamboline in plastica particolarmente originali, vasto assortimento di vestiti di ogni genere, viene fabbricata in due misure.
Lilli: Particularly original plastic dolls. Large assortment of dresses of all kind. Manufactured in two sizes.

Altri esemplari di bamboline Lilli.
Other specimens of Lilli dolls.

Ruth Handler, the "Mother of Barbie," as she herself likes to be known. Notwithstanding a few doubts about the legitimacy of that "maternity," it was surely her genial intuition to market Barbie with an ample and sophisticated wardrobe to be acquired separately.

to market musical toys, such as tiny pianos, guitars, and jack-in-the-boxes, and later branched out into miniature toy weapons such as rifles and pistols—all of which sold very well.

Ruth Handler wanted to initiate doll production as well but the low level of enthusiasm of the planners and designers—all men—along with evidence of other, more positive toy trends, ensured that her proposals were given little consideration.

The Rome company VeBi Giocattoli's 1961 catalog promoting Lilli testifies to the cross-cultural success and dissemination of this doll.

Reflecting back on Barbie's origins beyond their simple historical facts inevitably leads one to recognize missed opportunities, which is in some ways a testimony to the great creative impulses that are so often overlooked in the drive toward entrepreneurial success.

While the flourishing Mattel approached the 1950s with increasing profits, Ruth Handler did not abandon the idea of getting into the doll business; it was on her mind constantly. She watched her daughter, Barbara, and her little friends play contentedly for hours with magazine pictures and paper dolls, carefully cutting out clothes and accessories to dress them, and giving them adult roles

and professions. The power of a child's imagination to experiment with the possible roles of an adult future was not lost on Mrs. Handler. That influence, inherent in dolls since ancient times, is generated mainly through the opportunities the child has to change their clothes, thereby creating different characters with access to an otherwise unattainable adult universe.

*Above: This emblematic cover of the famous fashion magazine **Vogue** reiterates the stereotypical traits of the 1950s-style "face." The graphic enhancement of the photograph by Erwin Blumenfeld accents the essential elements of this look—the dramatically arched eyebrow, the eyeliner used to elongate the eye upward, and the full, well-defined, scarlet-red lips. The closeup of a Barbie Number One's face in the inset faithfully represents this prevailing aesthetic.*

Facing page: Barbie changed her image for the first time in 1961, flaunting a new hairdo called the "Bubble Cut," a style that is cut short and pouffed up.

The fact that her daughter's make-believe play depicted men, women, juveniles, and young children—images instinctively invested with manifold meanings—clearly showed Ruth Handler the enormous potential in this kind of imaginary play, something she considered fundamental to a proper childhood. In her mind, there was a need to render that play experience three-dimensionally. By creating a doll with adult features, one that could accomplish the same functions as the paper dolls but without the limitations of fragile, two-dimensional cutouts, Ruth Handler raised child's play to a new level.

According to the biographical material available on Mrs. Handler, she already had an exact image of the ideal modern doll, so she was able to describe it precisely to the designers in an effort to get production under way. The traits she had in mind are early evidence of the best-known features of Barbie as we know her—long and tapered legs, slender waist, buxom chest, distinctive facial details, and polished finger- and toenails. Even with such precise planning, and however carefully its commercial potential was intuited, the idea initially met with considerable resistance at Mattel, especially in light of the high costs forecasted for the new product launch. Such concerns no doubt disguised a certain skepticism about producing a doll with such explicitly adult features. A few years would pass before the dream could come true, and the turning point came with the Handler family's European vacation during the summer of 1956.

Lilli and Barbie

In Lucerne, Switzerland, Ruth Handler saw a doll in the window of a toy shop that perfectly matched the one she had in mind. Dreams soon turned into reality, taking shape under the curious and investigative eyes of Mrs. Handler and her daughter Barbara.

The doll in question was named Lilli and measured 11½ inches tall. Made of rigid plastic, she simulated a young blond woman, long-limbed and shapely in a way that evoked the buxom Brigitte Bardot. When Ruth Handler discovered her, Lilli already had a history and was enjoying great success. She originated in a comic strip designed by Reinhard Beuthien that appeared in June of 1952 in the German newspaper *Bild Zeitung*. The strip told lightly comic tales that were often punctuated by mildly sordid double entendres.

27

Top left: Impeccable in the "Tuxedo" outfit, Barbie's boyfriend Ken appeared on the American market in 1961. First produced with flocked fiber blond or brunette hair, he was later made with hair that was molded in vinyl and painted. Ken also hit the market with a large wardrobe.

Near left: Barbie's friend Midge, in production after 1963, wears the "Sorority Meeting" dress (1962–63).

The main character was Lilli, a lovely and sexy blond girl, who was busy keeping her many admirers at bay. Her popular success was enough to warrant her evolution into a three-dimensional doll.

For sale initially in smoke shops, and eventually toy shops as well, Lilli mainly targeted an adult audience, for which she assumed the role of provocateur, and was never intended for children. The credit for her transformation from newsprint to plastic went to Max Weissbrodt, the designer who perfected the prototype for the German firm

Hausser Elastolin, of Neustad, active in toy production since 1904, while 3M Dolls produced her clothing under the leadership of Martah Maar, mother of Rolf Hausser.

The first *Bild* Lilli appeared on the German market on August 12, 1955 and sold at 19.90 marks for the tallest version. It was later exported to other European countries and distributed in the United States as well. The doll was then marketed in a smaller, 7-inch version, again packaged in a cylindrical box of light, transparent plastic. Inside, she stood on a pedestal over the words "Bild Lilli" alternating with the red logo of the *Bild Zeitung* newspaper. Each Lilli wore just one dress from the many in her wardrobe, and the outfits were not sold separately. What's more, she was packaged with a miniature edition of the newspaper that appeared to be constructed completely around her character, dedicating the front page to many photographs of her.

The complex events that followed Ruth Handler's meeting with her ideal doll would finally set her own doll project in motion at Mattel. The differently dressed Lilli dolls purchased during the European vacation became the focus of study for the company's creative staff. Mattel acquired the patent and necessary rights; every technical detail of the doll was deconstructed and analyzed, and eventually integrated with current American tastes and fashions. Lilli dolls were the pattern onto which the original model of Barbie was slowly superimposed.

Left: "Barbie Fashion Queen" (1963). With her hair molded and pulled back, this Barbie can wear three different wigs sold with the doll. Below: The new hairdo "Swirl Pony-tail" was conceived by Jean Ann Burger in 1964.

FASHION QUEEN™ *Barbie*®

29

The many difficulties that followed, especially during the vinyl molding phase, caused considerable delay. Frequent trips to Japan were necessary to investigate numerous manufacturers there that specialized in the production of these materials at a more acceptable price. New players came onto the scene at Mattel during those early years whose professionalism would forever be associated with the growth of the company. Among them, Frank Nakamura was a key figure in developing relations between Mattel and Japan, and he is forever linked to the adventure that was the creation of the first Barbie. Another important figure was Charlotte Johnson, the young stylist who in 1956 started her auspicious collaboration with Mattel to conceive and design Barbie's legendary wardrobe. Between 1957 and 1964, the production of Barbie dolls, clothing, and accessories expanded to Hong Kong and Korea.

Barbie Arrives

Barbie—the name inspired by that of the Handlers' daughter, Barbara Joyce—officially debuted on the American market in March 1959 at New York City's American Toy Fair. Unaware of the future that awaited her, Barbie was buttressed by the commercial aptitude and insights of Ruth Handler, a shrewd believer in her innovatory potential.

Presented as a "teen-age fashion model," she was widely touted in the Mattel catalogs as "a new kind of doll from real life," with the serial number 850, measuring 11½ inches tall, and available in blond or brunette. Boxed in a pretty white carton illustrated on the outside with dress designs from the collection, she wore a black-and-white-striped jersey bathing suit and was accessorized with her celebrated white sunglasses with blue lenses, high-heeled black shoes, gold-hoop earrings, a pedestal on which to

support her, and the ubiquitous little catalog illustrating a variety of models that could be purchased at prices ranging from one to five dollars per package.

The Mattel logo and the name "Barbie," written in its distinctive script and printed on all point-of-purchase packaging, guaranteed the product and protected it from imitation. The doll also carried an imprint at the small of her back that was stamped directly onto the vinyl during the molding process:

Barbie™
Pats. Pend.
© MCMLVIII
by
Mattel
Inc.

This patent was submitted in 1958 and maintained the same trademark, sometimes using Arabic numbers for the date in place of the Roman numerals, until it was modified in 1966. Buyers met the doll with only moderate enthusiasm at first, perhaps troubled by the doll's adult features that were so alien to those of the usual innocuous baby dolls and little girls; she invited a certain caution. But these hesitations could not get the better of what already portended to be an unprecedented commercial phenomenon. During 1959, more than 351,000 Barbie dolls were sold at the price of three dollars apiece, a victory largely due to the ingenious idea of promoting the doll on television during the popular "Mickey Mouse Club" show. However,

NEW!

HER LEGS REALLY BEND

#1060

MISS *Barbie*®

Teen-Age Fashion Model

Her lifelike legs *really* bend!
Her eyes open and close!
Complete fashion wig wardrobe
with 3 wigs and wig stand!
Comes with simple-to-snap-
together Lawn Swing & Planter!
Miss Barbie is dressed in chic
pink swimsuit and fringed cap;
has a gold stand. $9.00

Facing page: Promotional catalogs from 1960–63. Useful for advertising Barbie's wardrobe, they were always included in product packaging.

Above: Advertisement for "Miss

Barbie" (1964), the first doll with bendable legs and moveable eyes.

Right: Barbie's little sister Skipper, produced from 1964 on, wears the "Me 'N My Doll" outfit (1964–66).

31

*The year 1964 saw
the introduction of
Allan, Midge's
"boyfriend," who had
the same body mold
as Ken so he could
share his wardrobe.
He is seen here in the
"Rovin Reporter"
outfit (1965).*

Ruth Handler's instinct to market the doll with a big wardrobe full of clothes and accessories sold separately was clearly the real trump card.

Beyond having transformed Lilli into Barbie and given her a fresh, previously inconceivable market appeal, Mattel could not hide Barbie's European roots. If Barbie Number One and Lilli are examined side by side, the similarities between the two dolls are remarkable. The bodies are identical in shape and proportions, as is the mechanism for moving the legs; the shoulder joint was simplified into a hinge rather than elastic for Barbie. The shoes were different, in that Lilli's feet were molded in the shape of a high-heeled shoe and painted black, while Barbie had bare feet in an arched position that made it easy to slip on different pairs of high-heeled shoes. Among other varying details were Lilli's painted earrings, always in black, whereas Barbie's pierced ears permitted different styles to be inserted and coordinated with her dresses. In addition, her fingernails were more finely contoured and her toenails were polished red. The two dolls' facial features and profiles were altogether comparable, with the slight variation of Lilli's more elongated face. The makeup on Barbie's face varied slightly by conforming to the dictates of American fashion. The deep red mouth was carefully shaped and widened; the eyebrows were subtly arched; and the eyelids held blue eye shadow over contoured eyeliner. The comparison between Barbie Number One's face and Erwin Blumenfeld's splendid photographic portrait (see p. 26) is remarkable. His retouched photo became the cover of the January 1950

American *Vogue*, and continues to fascinate us even today in its depiction of the absolute essence of female beauty as ordained in the 1950s.

Credit for the final model of Barbie Number One's face belongs to the sculptor Kohei Suzuki. Eyes that averted their glance downward, with a distinctive white sparkle in the iris, were similar in both Lilli and Barbie. While each sported the popular ponytail hairdo, Barbie had short, curly bangs and Lilli's hair was pulled back but for a single curl over a severe widow's peak. The hair on Barbie's head was inserted by a familiar method of sewing it onto soft vinyl, while Lilli's hair was inserted along the seam, held up by the pressure exerted by a screw holding the two pieces of her head together. The two dolls could stand upright if positioned on their respective pedestals; studs on the individual bases were inserted into either a singular hole under Lilli's foot, or, in Barbie's case, by two holes reinforced by little metal cylinders. Lilli was made of a rigid plastic material, while Barbie was formed of various types of vinyl that were soft for the head, rigid for

After 1965, Barbie showed off bendable knees and sported the short new bobbed cut called "American Girl." She is seen here wearing the "Modern Art" ensemble (1965), complete with a painting and a gallery flyer.

the bust, and moderately soft for the arms that, like the legs, were solid.

So Barbie's true novelty was not found in her general appearance, which was a revised version of Lilli's, nor in the small aesthetic and technical improvements that would continually be added over time, moving her away from the look of the original prototype, but never very far from the concept of the fashion model/doll who could be endlessly transformed by means of her constantly changing wardrobe—a doll to inspire endless imagination and desire.

A Barbie in Constant Evolution

In the years to come, Barbie was continually altered to tailor her more carefully to market expectations and to improve her competitive edge. Barbie Number Two appeared at the end of 1959 and differed from Number One only in that she no longer had holes in her feet to attach her to her pedestal, a system that had required perforating her shoes to match her feet. Positioning the doll upright in this fashion was probably too costly and complex, and it was soon replaced by a new pedestal with a wire that supported the doll under her arms—decidedly easier and cheaper.

A truly significant change in Barbie's body came in 1967, when the doll was issued with her newly bendable waist and called, aptly, "Twist 'N Turn."

34

Barbie Number Three appeared in 1960 with some changes in her facial makeup: her eyes were blue, eyebrows more horizontal, and her eye shadow became a mix of blue and brown. The subsequent Number Four doll had a look generally the same as Number Three, but the color of the vinyl skin changed, yielding a darker tint than the pallid color used up to that point. A succession of experiments in the early years of production strived for a vinyl with optimal plasticity and chromaticism before a suitable formula was found. Many of the dolls fabricated in this experimental phase later showed deterioration, with a partial or total discoloration and an oily, translucent cast to the face.

A special innovation appeared in 1961 when Barbie got a new hairdo. Alongside the famous ponytail, Larry Germaine of Universal Studios created a short cut that was more modern and fashionable. Baptized the "Bubble Cut" by Americans, it consisted of short layers pouffed out over the neck and ears, and had a decidedly chic air.

That year also marked the production of the first dolls with red hair.

Barbie's boyfriend Ken, named after the Handlers' son Kenneth Robert, made his debut in 1961, taking his place in the limelight beside his already-famous partner. He was furnished with a smart, masculine wardrobe that was richly tailored and perfectly appointed for escorting Barbie through the numerous sophisticated and/or sportive engagements of their "life."

"Talking Busy Barbie" (1972). From 1968 on, Barbie talked. Thanks to a mechanism activated by a pull cord at the nape of her neck, she could say six complete sentences.

Barbie Embarks for Europe

A turning point in Barbie's international "career" was her 1961 arrival in London, where she was exhibited for the first time in a showcase of American toy products. From this British metropolis her voyage of conquest advanced to Paris, the fashion capital, where she was presented in 1963 at the "Salon du Jouet." Other countries followed, where she continued to spread the word of Barbie, officially assuming her place in the European toy market.

Barbie's best friend Midge was added to the growing family in 1963. A very popular doll, she offered a sweet and smiling face accentuated by freckles on her cheeks. The prototype for her body was the same one used for Barbie so Midge could wear the same clothes as her friend. From then on the dolls were marketed in tandem.

"Barbie Fashion Queen" was another clever invention that year, consisting of a Barbie doll whose hair was molded in vinyl directly onto her head and held back in a ribbon so that any of three wigs packaged with the doll could be worn over it.

More changes debuted in 1964; while Barbie continued her global dissemination, landing in Italy with

her rich wardrobe in tow, "Miss Barbie" was marketed in America, the first doll in the series with moveable, closeable eyes and legs that bent at the knee. Conceived by Dick May, the inventor and patent-holder for bendable legs, the new doll also reintroduced the "Fashion Queen" series of wigs in new colors and styles, enabling a little girl to have three dolls in one.

On the subject of hair, the classic Barbie with the ponytail was modified and modernized in 1964 thanks to the stylistic participation of Jean Ann Burger, who in 1963 had conceived the new hairdo, "Swirl Ponytail." The curls on the forehead had disappeared, leaving a band of smooth hair combed sideways across the forehead and then caught up in the ponytail. For her face, newer makeup abandoned the flaming-red lipstick in favor of pastel and pearlized colors, and even an opaque white. This new look was a very becoming update of the fashions of the time.

Some new characters produced in 1964–65 included Skipper, Barbie's little sister; Allan, Midge's boyfriend, whose height and body were the same proportions as Ken's; and Skooter and Ricky, two new friends of Skipper. From 1965 on, Barbie and all her friends had legs that bent at the knee.

Barbie's next short hairstyle, again created by Jean Ann Burger, presented her with a sleek, straight cut with bangs, somewhat resembling a helmet. This new "do," decidedly modern, sportive, and elegant at the same time, is known among collectors as "American Girl."

In the following years, the enhancements and continuing discoveries that changed

"Talking Julia" (1969) introduced the television character played by the African-American actress Diahann Carroll (photo below), who was extremely popular that year. The refined facial resemblance took advantage of careful modeling and facial decoration. She wore a "palazzo pajama" in gold and silver lamé.

17

18

19

20

21

22

the face of Barbie and her friends, helping to maintain their characteristic fashion-forward images, followed one another in rapid succession in the endless race to keep up with the demands of consumers.

Among the most salient innovations was the introduction in 1966 of Barbie's cousin Francie, whose adolescent features and youthful wardrobe brought a modernity inspired by the latest London fashions. The "Color Magic Barbie" was fairly radical, yet vastly amusing: created under the inventive imagination of Ralph Dunn, this doll could change the color of her hair and of the dress she was wearing.

In 1967, Barbie's facial features and makeup changed completely. Synthetic eyelashes were applied onto larger painted eyes, and her hair became longer, flowing loosly over her shoulders and gathered up by a little ribbon on the top of her head. With a patented torso that could swivel and rotate, this new doll was dubbed "Twist 'N Turn."

She was so novel that Mattel promoted her as the beginning of a new Barbie generation in a massive commercial launch offering the "Twist 'N Turn" doll at a reduced price—only $1.50—if customers traded in an older Barbie at the time of purchase. Mattel collected a vast number of used dolls—then considered out of date—during this promotional event and donated them to charity.

In 1968, Barbie dolls were able to speak. The new "Talking Barbie" dazzled her fans with six sentences indicative of her daily concerns: "What shall I wear to

This page:
A 1963 catalog of
the Società Editrice
Giochi, Barbie's
Italian distributor
during that period.
The models in Series
1600 were pictured
with an Italianized
version of their
names and a sale
price in lire.

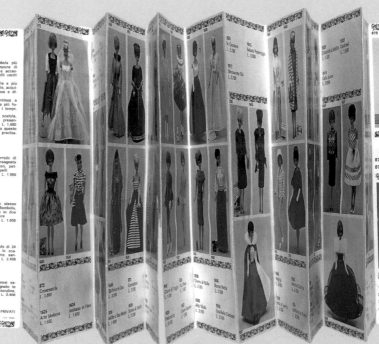

1

2

3

4

5

6

1 and 27. *Bob Mackie Jewel Series, "Diamond," 1997*

2 and 21. *"Starlight Waltz Barbie," 1995*

3 and 16. *"Midnight Gala," 1995*

4. *"Water Lili," 1997*

5 and 18. *Great Eras Series, "French Lady," 1997*

6 and 24. *"All Decked Out," 1997*

7. *"Uptown Chic Barbie," 1991*

8 and 22. *"Sugar Plum Fairy," 1997*

13

14

15

16

7

8

9

10

11

12

9 and 30. *Bob Mackie Jewel Series, "Gold,"* 1991

10 and 15. *"City Slickers,"* 1997

11. *"Court Favorite,"* 1997

12. *"Perfectly Suited Giftset,"* 1997

13. *Bob Mackie Barbie, "Empress Bride,"* 1992

14 and 29. *American Stories Series, "Patriot,"* 1997

17. *Bob Mackie Jewel Series, "Emerald,"* 1997

19. *Bob Mackie Jewel Series, "Amethyst,"* 1997

20. *"Cinderella,"* 1997

23. *"Romantic Interlude,"* 1997

25. *Great Eras Series, "Chinese Empress,"* 1997

26. *"Midnight Princess,"* 1997

28. *"Barbie Loves Elvis Giftset,"* 1997

28

30

23

24

25

26

27

29

the Prom?"; "I have a date tonight"; "Would you like to go shopping?"; "Stacey and I are having tea"; "Let's have a costume party" and "I love being a fashion model." Along with the American model, Mattel distributed a Spanish-speaking version designed especially for that market.

The famous American actress, Farrah Fawcett-Majors, who inspired new features for "Barbie Superstar" (1977).

That same year, Barbie's first African-American friend, Christie, was added to the lineup of friends and relatives already on the market. Mattel also opened a branch office in Italy in order to avoid the middleman and distribute Barbie products themselves. The chosen locale was Oleggio Castello, in the Novara region, and it is still active today, specializing in the production of Barbie doll accessories.

Thanks to its expansion of market territories as a result of increased product demand, Mattel began in 1968 to look beyond Japan for new factory sites where they might keep production costs low. New plants in Mexico, Korea, Taiwan, and the Philippines were soon to follow.

Mattel continued to forge ahead with fresh ideas and innovations for the doll and her line of accessories, among them the addition of a pantheon of new characters in the Barbie clan and countless enhancements of Barbie's facial expression. Among the latter, one of the most famous was created by the sculptor Joyce Clark in the shape of "Barbie Superstar" (1977), which is still around today. She flashes the unmistakable smile

and the luminous eyes inspired by the then-popular actress Farrah Fawcett-Majors, a celebrated heroine of the television series "Charlie's Angels."

These were only some of the basic stages that marked the evolution of Barbie. The number and variety of models introduced, along with the countless series of accessories that fill her world, could be the subject of endless lists and related discussion. Many such careful studies have been published and should also be referenced, if only to enhance one's grasp of the richly detailed, fantastical world of Barbie from 1959 on. We will conclude this historical overview of Barbie with a few curious details about her.

Barbie dolls have been sold in more than 140 countries, at a rate of two every second across the globe. Since 1959, nearly one billion outfits have been produced, including more than one billion pairs of shoes. Each year about 150 different doll models are brought to the international market; in Italy alone about three million Barbie dolls are sold annually. From the data provided by Mattel, we can ascertain that the

business of Barbie continues to multiply each year at a staggering rate.

More than a Simple Doll

The arrival of this doll in Europe was immediately followed by incremental jumps in the index of distribution to the juvenile public. The index met and bypassed 80 percent and, in some countries, achieved a 90 percent penetration. Italy, for example, holds by far the record on this European index at 99 percent, a figure equal to that seen in the United States. When 99 individuals out of 100 (in this case, girls from 3 to 10 years of age) possess at least one piece of the product in question, that product can truly be called a marketing phenomenon. On this basis we can affirm that Barbie dolls and their accessories constitute the most spectacular marketing phenomenon to hit the toy market in the last forty years.

We would be hard pressed at this point to consider her as nothing more than a simple doll.

"Barbie Superstar" (1977) represents a later aesthetic in her continuing evolution as the ideal of feminine beauty, achieved as always with precision.

45

Models taken from real life and, more precisely, from the all-American reality that is the world of the movies, continually inspire Barbie's aesthetic and commercial evolution.

Barbie

1959 and Haute Couture

Am I too daring? I ask this question with absolute sincerity because in the last few months several influential women have told me maybe I am. I have been accused of having terrible taste in clothes, of showing off too much and of making vulgar use of my figure on a lot of social occasions.

(Marilyn Monroe, "Am I Too Daring?" in *Modern Screen*, July 1952)

Facing page: Barbie wearing one of Christian Dior's most famous designs, a synthesis of the "New Look" style launched in 1947. Left: A photograph of the original design.

This was how the celebrated actress started a brief chat about the way she dressed and about being so often the subject of both harsh disapproval and equally ardent approval. Clearly it wasn't easy to dress such an explosive body. It couldn't be contained in sheaths, whose seams always seemed close to bursting. All of this incited both the moral indignation of proper ladies and the pining glances of men lost in their fantasies. Poor Marilyn, more hotly debated than other American divas because she stole hearts and became the object of men's more or less secret desires. She was a product for public consumption, a well-packaged shell of whom nothing more was required than that she display herself and cater to our private fantasy worlds. Her personal sentiments and professionalism were of little interest in comparison.

A C C E S S O R I E S

The hat box from the "Commuter Set" outfit and the straw purse decorated with fruit from "Suburban Shopper." All of Barbie's ensembles produced from 1959 to 1966 were characterized by particularly refined accessories, enhancing the quality and originality of the garments.

Dolls embody that same kind of feminine beauty, which in the pre-feminist era was nothing more than a masculine ideal of perfection meant for entertainment and fantasy fulfillment—in other words, women as playthings.

Unlike Marilyn, Barbie is a real doll that plays at being a woman, and as such has since become, inevitably, a diva. However, in the eyes of some adults—those viewed by Barbie supporters as perhaps disillusioned or even misled—she gives form to the same desires aroused by the woman-as-object mentality, and it has been this way from the time she appeared; she is studied, abhorred, and also loved.

Love and hate surround her commercial success, sentiments that have kept pace with her active diffusion into the juvenile imagination. The developed, elegant body has been worshiped and shown off in endless combinations by the wardrobe that has continued to grow and evolve in perfect conjunction with changes in fashion. Despite the critical stance of feminist mothers, intellectuals, and activists in the protests of the 1970s, who themselves remained immune to Barbie's powers of persuasion, these same women were forced to accept seeing their daughters squeeze their Barbie dolls in proud, loving possession. In recent years, Barbie has continued

These three designs — now rare collectibles — at once exhibit stylistic inventiveness and impressive sartorial quality. The outfits are "Roman Holiday," "Gay Parisienne," and "Easter Parade," all from 1959 and only produced that year. They are emblematic of a certain way of dressing that combined haute couture designs and fine accessories, evocative in their lines and careful color accents. The pervading tone lies somewhere between European — particularly French — and American tastes.

Left: An official photograph of Evita Peron, famous for her showy elegance, wearing a sumptuous evening gown representative of the "New Look."

Below: Doris Day wears a classic wool sweater coupled with a tweed skirt, a "girl next door" outfit very much in vogue during the 1950s and 1960s.

to be ostracized by experts of good breeding and etiquette, teachers, and sociologists, all of whom worry about the future of today's young girls who are subjected to what is in their eyes a very negative model of womanhood. Amidst the pros and cons, somewhere between exaltation and denigration, Barbie yet emerges unscathed, with valid support for her popularity and success, still surrounded after forty years with increasing pangs of nostalgia.

Barbie dolls are inseparable from the thousands of accessories that enrich their world, to the point

Barbie wears the
"Sweater Girl" outfit,
produced between
1959 and 1962, which
was so successful it
was introduced in
other colors and
combinations in the
years to come.

SWEATER GIRL
(without doll) #976
Sleeveless turtle-neck
sweater with matching
cardigan. Tailored
wrap-around flannel
skirt.
Knitting needles, yarns,
scissors in a bowl,
and Barbie's own
knitting book. Open-toe
pumps. The set,
$3.00

#976

As seen in the
original catalog
sketch, it is
accompanied by
various accessories.
A proper "uniform"
for legions of young
and not-so-young
women, this manner
of dress seemed
to convey an
incontrovertible,
squeaky-clean
morality.

FRIDAY NITE DATE
(without doll) #979
Powder blue corduroy
jumper with colorful felt
appliques. White blouse
and bouffant pettiskirt. Black
plastic shoes. Two plastic
coke tumblers with serving
tray and drinking straws.
The set, $2.50

questionable taste if that was the style of the day. On the contrary, the Mattel clothing designers shamelessly hedge their bets on the public reactions to fashion trends, incorporating them in the creative process. In a way, this enables Barbie to keep an open dialogue with her fans, enhancing her reach as a global phenomenon. Barbie does not predict fashion; she seconds its whims and transforms them into an internationally unifying game. From ready-to-wear to haute couture, Barbie's designers take inspirations, strip them of pretense, and transform them into believable ensembles. It could be said that no other object transforms intangible concepts—in this case, of fashion—into substantive products with comparable success.

To observe and reflect on this form and quantity of clothes production, we must summarize the decade between Barbie's introduction in 1959 and the year

where, nowadays, when Barbie is mentioned, more than a plain vinyl doll comes to mind. Instead, there are images of luxurious houses, cars, campers, and motorbikes accompanied by an entourage of friends, boyfriends, little sisters, animals and, above all, a wardrobe that not even Jacqueline Kennedy, Evita Peron, or Imelda Marcos could dream up or presume to own.

The Significance of the Clothes

It is Barbie's wardrobe, in fact, that now warrants a critical eye in our contemplation of this icon of the twentieth century, as we set aside the protests that fall outside an analysis of the precise historical period of fashion so beautifully portrayed by these minuscule outfits.

Barbie's huge wardrobe never shied away from

To satisfy every expectation of her customers, Barbie does not shy away from taking on the most diverse roles, from fresh-faced little girl to femme fatale and ultra-sophisticated Park Avenue society matron.

In keeping with a youthful idea in the guise of simplicity, the "Friday Nite Date" outfit, produced from 1960 to 1964, dresses Barbie for a quiet date with Ken, maybe in the backyard, where they will be served two definitively nonalcoholic drinks.

SUBURBAN SHOPPER
(without doll) #969
Novelty cotton-and-lace suntop dress has zipper back. Cute cartwheel strawhat, and fruit-filled tote bag. Necklace, pumps. Telephone, too! The set, $2.50.

#969

The "Suburban Shopper" outfit in the blue version from 1959, rechristened "Busy Morning" (facing page).

54

1970. The steady output of clothes and accessories that followed in those years combined impressive technical qualities and endless creativity, elements that were the foundation of Barbie's success. However, all was not sound within Mattel, as market fluctuations, company administrative problems, and changes in management ultimately led Ruth Handler to quit her presidency in 1974.

Stylistically, we will see that Barbie has her deepest roots in the fashions of the 1950s, at a time when the world was struggling to assimilate the post–World War II realities of everyday life. The period of sacrifice and rationing was at an end, and countries on both sides of the Atlantic began to have new hope for a prosperous future.

The "New Look"

The city of Paris sought to reassert its dominance as the capital of style and fashion—a dominance that even cutting-edge New York City had to reckon with—and this was accomplished in part by Christian Dior's famous fashion show in February 1947. In one fell swoop, his revolutionary "New Look" obliterated the prewar competition by touting an

image that was emphatically feminine and luxurious. In 1984 Natalia Aspesi wrote an article about the fashion era between 1948 and 1968 stating, "Women rediscovered their taste for high-end glamour with the 'New Look.' The waist was narrow, and skirts were full, rounded and resumed a length 8 inches from the floor. It was a fashion for *grandes dames*, and among the first to frequent the fashion houses were the Duchess of Windsor, Evita Peron, Princess Liliana of Belgium, and Baroness Alain de Rothschild. Even for daywear women had the impetus to look like queens, and everyone, even those women who could only admire the garments from afar, wanted them."

The lives of fashion-conscious Americans were soon suffused with that taste, and it became especially prevalent among movie stars and society doyennes who served as models for the general public. Haute couture details were incorporated into Barbie's dresses by Charlotte Johnson, a designer from the Chouinard Art School in Los Angeles, who worked on the first series of twenty-two designs in 1959. According to fashion guidelines of today, we would

1959

The Age of Innocence, her celebrated 1920 novel, in which the main character maintains that it was considered vulgar to dress in the latest fashion, and young women were instructed instead to put away for two years dresses that came right from Paris. This tradition was reinforced in the highest levels of society, and inevitably reflected in the world of Barbie, whose appearance was intended by her creators to be upper class, at least in comparison to her

Left: Grace Kelly, known for her exquisite beauty and elegance, wears a dress from the film High Society (1955).

Below: An illustration for the "Plantation Belle" design (1959).

consider these outfits outmoded even when observed in their historical context. Barbie's wardrobe, like most clothing lines, naturally took more inspiration from the past than the present, and Mattel's creative staff had a good eye for stereotypes—in this case, the luxuries of French fashion.

In late nineteenth-century America, it was not considered chic to wear clothes that were fresh from the fashion houses. Edith Wharton wrote about this in

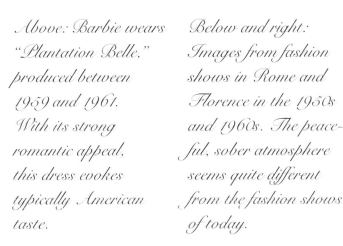

Above: Barbie wears "Plantation Belle," produced between 1959 and 1961. With its strong romantic appeal, this dress evokes typically American taste.

Below and right: Images from fashion shows in Rome and Florence in the 1950s and 1960s. The peaceful, sober atmosphere seems quite different from the fashion shows of today.

audience. Such a notion was admittedly snobbish in a modern context, and it was soon overshadowed by the influences of domestic fashion and the world of Hollywood movies.

An example of this American influx was the "Sweater Girl" outfit (#976, 1959–62), composed of a gray flannel skirt with a cardigan sweater and shell in reddish-orange wool, accessorized with balls of wool and knitting needles. The ensemble recalled Lana Turner's "skirt-and-sweater" appeal, or the fresh-faced, girl-next-door looks of June Allyson and Doris Day. Another example, the "Suburban Shopper" (#969, 1959–64) was a sundress with shoulder straps in a blue cotton print striped with bands of white lace. It had a narrow waist and a full skirt cut just below the knee. Accessorized by a wide-brimmed straw hat, a bag of fruit, high-heeled sandals, and a white telephone, the ensemble was a classic Dior look. Cinematic references called to mind the freshness of the blond and beautiful Grace Kelly in the film, *High Society* (1955).

1959

"Gay Parisienne"
(1959) will always
be one of the chicest
dresses in the history of
Barbie's wardrobe.
58 Characterized by the
so-called balloon-line
skirt, conceived by
Hubert de Givenchy,
and elegantly
accessorized, the
ensemble is finished
with couture details
like the bow at
the back.

On the facing page
we see a similar
design photographed
in Venice.

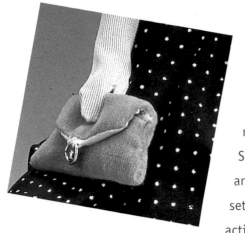

"Plantation Belle" (#966, 1959–61) was designed as a party dress in the romantic era of the Southern plantations and grand houses that set the scene for the activities of the capricious Scarlet O'Hara. It had a fitted, scoop-necked bodice, and full round skirt, and was made of light-pink tulle lined in pink cotton, trimmed with flounces of white bobbin lace. The outfit also included a wide-brimmed hat with ribbons; a white crinoline of tulle and nylon; a straw purse in the shape of a bucket; short white gloves; high-heeled sandals; and pink pearl jewelry.

Roman Holiday

"Roman Holiday" (#968, produced only in 1959) was one of the most evocative designs of Barbie's wardrobe and is considered a true rarity among collectors today. An elegant outfit composed of a dress and overcoat, the one-piece, knee-length sheath has a scoop-necked bodice in red and white stripes above a blue skirt, and a glossy white plastic belt with a cotton buckle accentuating the waist. Sewn in the same striped fabric, the overcoat had a straight line and was only slightly longer than the skirt, with three-quarter-length sleeves, spherical gold buttons, and a collar with wide lapels. Accessories included an envelope-shaped clutch purse in shiny white plastic containing a tiny pink comb, a compact and matching brush with the initial "B," a small handkerchief, and black glasses with a case; short white gloves; and black sandals. With the

sharp color contrast, the outfit was extremely chic, combining a tailored elegance with a touch of American eccentricity.

Not even Barbie could resist the charm of Rome, like the multitude of more or less famous stars who arrived from America when the studio Cinecittà opened its doors to some of Hollywood's biggest productions. The attractions of the Italian capital were endless; its historical romance, with just a hint of novelty, was quickly transformed into timeless fashions, which were then exported to anxiously awaiting celebrities. Natalia Aspesi, in the essay cited above, evoked this atmosphere effectively: "Hollywood rained down on the Tiber to shoot its historical

films, and the stars came, mythical and gorgeous. Enchanted by the city, they ate, they gained weight, they fell in love, and they found in Italian high fashion that voluptuous and somewhat vulgar splendor to complement their stardom. . . . But it was the Fontana sisters who successfully infiltrated American cinema. They had already seen great success, spreading a passion for Italian luxuries all over the world . . . but now *Roman Holiday* and *Quo Vadis?* were being shot in Rome and these sisters, Micol, Zoe, and Giovanna, understood better than anyone else that from then on it was the film divas, and not the stoic aristocrats, who would best advertise fashion."

So it was during these first years of the 1950s that Italian fashion began to feel the benefits of this peaceful invasion by such rich and spectacular women as Barbara Stanwyck, Deborah Kerr, Audrey Hepburn, Elizabeth Taylor, and Ava Gardner; partly in thanks to them, it began to take its first few steps toward autonomy from the dominant styles of Paris. The now-famous fashion show by Giovan Battista Giorgini, on February 12, 1951 in Florence, had already confirmed this trend. Umberto

Tirelli wrote about it in 1984: "We spent hours walking on the beach at Des Bains. 'Bista' (Giorgini) was thinking out loud about ways to launch Italian high fashion after years of being in the shadows of French haute couture. . . . His logic was simple: why submit to Paris when in Italy we had the best textiles, the best seamstresses, and the most talented tailors? On February 12, 1951, Antonelli, Simonetta, Fonata, Fabiani, Schubert, Marucelli, Veneziani, Noberasco, and Wanna put on a spectacular show in Giorgini's beautiful house in Florence. It was sort of a declaration of independence from the French. That's how Italian fashion was born."

Parisian Origins

As a miniature diva, Barbie represented all designers, assuming a more universal role and freer image that did not indulge obvious preferences. Thus, if she enjoyed the romantic fascination of a "Roman holiday"—just like Audrey Hepburn in the famous film of 1954—she also did not hesitate to take advantage of the equally charming Paris.

Among the most successful designs in the 1959 collection, "Gay Parisienne" (#964, only produced that year) once again represented an international elegance. It was a short, strapless evening dress with a form-fitting bodice finished with a bow at the back, and a balloon-line skirt with another bow at the knee. Made of blue rayon taffeta with tiny white polka dots, the ensemble was completed by a veil of tulle over swept-up hair; a white rabbit-fur stole lined in satin; a beige velvet bag; long white evening gloves; blue sandals; and a pearl necklace and earrings.

Facing page: "Easter Parade" (1959), with an elegant overcoat in black faille.

Barbie wears the "Evening Splendour" outfit, produced from 1959 to 1964. One of the most famous and widely sold garments in the 900 series, it is composed of an elegant strapless dress and an overcoat lined in light-blue satin with real fur finishes. The precious metallic-gold brocade fabric, made in Japan, accents the utterly American glamour of this design, which was apparently meant for attending the sophisticated cocktail parties immortalized so well by the celebrated film comedies set in 1950s New York. At left, the original sketch.

61

COMMUTER SET
(without doll) #916
Two-piece jersey box-jacket
suit. Skirt has side zipper.
Two blouses: classic nylon
check; dressy v-back white
satin. White gloves, crystal
rope beads and bracelet.
Petal-cloche hat; shoes.
Fashion model's hatbox. The
set. $3.50.

#916

"Commuter Set," in
production from 1959
to 1960, is one of the
most traditional suits
in Barbie's closet.
Clearly borrowing
from the taste of Coco
Chanel, it incorporates
the linear simplicity of
her inimitable style
with accessories like
the long, double-strand
necklace and bracelet
and the eccentric floral
hat, which adds an
intense splash of color.

Among the many silhouettes that characterized fashion during the 1950s—including the princess line, the tulip, the A-line, and the sack dress—the bubble dress that Hubert De Givenchy debuted mid-decade is undoubtedly one of the more curious and uncomfortable designs ever produced by the all-male couturiers of the day. Regardless, this minuscule design was a huge hit, and it remains one of the rarest and most sought-after collectibles among those Barbie fans able to pay very high prices for additions to their collections.

"Easter Parade" (#971, produced only in 1959), an elegant ensemble of dress and overcoat, is also among the group of designs now considered rare. The one-piece, tight dress is sleeveless and has a wide boat neck—rounded in

In this photograph from Life magazine, dated March 25, 1946, the elegance of this young lady's outfit becomes a mirror and a model for Barbie's "Commuter Set," which is similar in design and conception, including the striking hatbox carried like a purse.

shoulder and gathered for greater volume. The wide collar can also be worn turned up, and the sleeves are elbow length. Bows are applied to the side pockets, adding a hint of haute couture. The accessories include a black netted bow hair clip; a shiny black patent bag; short white gloves; black heels; and a pearl necklace and earrings.

The subtle elegance of this suit is reminiscent of the top Parisian fashion houses. The influence of the great designer Cristobal Balenciaga seems obvious, especially in the light overcoat with its references to the sumptuous taffeta evening capes made in the mid-1950s. The masterful tailoring made ample use of fabric and soft lines emphasized by gathers and darts in the back.

"Evening Splendour" (#961, 1959–64) was an outfit truly befitting the wealthy New York society ladies of Fifth and Park Avenues, who passed their days juggling appointments and shopping with dreams to "marry a millionaire." Made in metallic-gold brocade with a small floral pattern of ferns and corollas, the precious Japanese fabric had the added luxury of brown imitation mink fur bordering the sleeves and the hat. It consisted mainly of two elements: the form-fitting dress, cut low and strapless, and hemmed just below the knee; and the slender overcoat, narrow at the hem, with elbow-

front with a "v" at the back—and is emphasized by a soft rolled collar that ends in two pointed tabs. Falling just below the knee, the fabric is a cotton print with charming multicolored apples on a black background. The overcoat in black rayon taffeta has a full, bell-shaped line, open in front with no buttons; the back panels are stitched at the

NIGHTY-NEGLIGEE SET

(without doll) #965
Luxurious full-length tricot gown, Grecian bodice with embroidered flower. Matching peignoir of finely tucked tricot with embroidered pocket. Toy stuffed dog for Barbie's bed. The set, $3.00.

#965

Facing page: Coco Chanel, with an ever-present cigarette between her lips, personally fits one of her famous suits on actress Romy Schneider. These two women, so different in background, sensibility, and career, are brought together by the popular success of their respective strong personalities and their love of fashion.

FLORAL PETTICOAT

(without doll) #921
Crisp nylon sheer petticoat, all-over embroidered with pastel floral design and matching panties. Strapless bra, vanity mirror, comb, brush set. Complete, $1.25.

FASHION UNDERGARMENTS

(without doll) #919
Tricot half-slip has fluted flounce to match panties. Embroidered tricot girdle and strapless bra. The set, $1.00.

#921

#919

Above: At left, "Lovely Lingerie pak," in production between 1964 and 1967; at right, "Nighty-Negligee Set," from 1959 to 1964.

Left: Sketch from a 1960 catalog showing two Barbie lingerie sets: "Fashion Undergarments," 1959–62, and "Floral Petticoat," 1959–63.

length sleeves and a pointed collar. Inside it was lined in pale-blue cotton sateen. Among the accessories were a little purse of sky-blue corduroy lined in white containing a tiny handkerchief; a headpiece in pearls and fur; brown high-heels; short white gloves; and matching pearl necklace and earrings.

The House of Chanel

One of the most important events in the history of fashion in the 1950s was the reopening in Paris of the Chanel atelier in 1954. Closed during the Second World War, it swiftly made a huge comeback, clearly not having lost any of its prewar notoriety. The designs of Coco Chanel, who was then in her sixties, offered her prestigious clientele an understated and refined elegance in stark contrast to the opulent, almost costume-like designs that were seen everywhere else. Always a nonconformist, she was decisive and secure in the choices she made to unify style and comfort, liberating women from the uncomfortable constraints of most haute couture. In her first postwar show, she introduced clean, loose lines that were simple, yet elegant.

Eliminating the whalebone corsets that, according to Chanel, made "the waist too narrow even for a wasp," she introduced her classic suits with the famous gold chains, part of the foundation of her timeless attire that has yet to fade alongside the fashions of today.

The press initially met Coco Chanel's insurgent ideas with a certain chill, dubbing her collection a flop. But it was her loyal clientele—tired of ostentatious luxury—who declared her a triumph. Natalia Aspesi wrote: "Luchino Visconti introduced Chanel to Romy Schneider, who became a passionate client and wore her creations in the film *Boccaccio '70*. Jacqueline Kennedy was wearing one of

A group of friends takes a break after a doubles tennis match. Barbie and Midge both wear the "Tennis Anyone?" outfit (1962–63), Ken wears "Time for Tennis" (1962–63), and Allan dons a sports outfit composed of several items from assorted "paks."

Chanel's pink suits on November 22, 1963, the day of the tragedy in Dallas, once again weaving fashion and history into a truly indelible image."

It was Chanel who inspired the "Commuter Set" outfit (#916, 1959–60), a suit of midnight-blue cotton jersey that faithfully re-creates the famous designs of Coco for Barbie. The suit came with two blouses, one in ivory satin for elegant occasions and the other in a cotton print with tiny blue checks and a buttoned little collar for daytime. A hat of three silk flowers, available in red or hot pink, lent a touch of eccentricity to the elegant sobriety of the suit. Black sandals, short white gloves, and a double-strand

Facing page: For a football party, Midge wears "Cheerleader" (1964–65), Allan "Campus Hero" (1961–64), Ken "Touchdown" (1963–65), and Barbie "Drum Majorette" (1964–65).

This page: The always sportive Barbie goes fishing dressed in the "Picnic Set" outfit (1959–61), with its big straw hat, a purse, and, naturally, the fishing rod with a fish already attached.

PICNIC SET
(without doll) #967—Checked gingham shirt with blue denim jeans, tailored with zipper fly. Wedge shoes and amusing straw hat. Picnic basket to carry the fish Barbie caught with her pole! Complete set, $2.50.

#967

Barbie is so versatile, she wears not only the trappings of a woman prone to society balls and formal affairs, but also those of an always impeccable housewife in front of the stove. The illustrated "Barbie-2 Outfit," produced from 1959 to 1962, displays the most stereotypical elements of women's cookware from a glossy magazine or a television food show.

BARBIE-Q OUTFIT

(without doll) #962
Cotton sunback dress
with Chef hat and apron.
Barbecue cooking
utensils and potholder.
Summer shoes. The
set. $2.00.

962

skirts, "Floral Petticoat" (#921, 1959–63); for sleepwear, "Sweet Dreams" (#973, 1959–63); and "Nighty-Negligee Set" (#965, 1959–64), a charming baby-doll set of nightgown with matching robe in traditional pink complete with pom-pom slippers; a toy stuffed dog; an alarm clock; a diary; and an apple for a midnight snack.

Sports and outdoor life were captured in three outfits very different in style and function. "Picnic Set" (#967, 1959–61) combined classic blue jeans with a red-and-white-checked blouse; a straw hat and purse; platform sandals made of cork; and the requisite fishing pole with a colored fish already on the hook—just in case! For boat trips, there was the "Resort Set" (#963, 1959–62), with a red sailor shirt; a sweater in blue and white stripes; white shorts and hat; cork-heeled shoes; and a gold charm bracelet. A weekend in the snow-covered mountains required "Winter Holiday" (#975, 1959–63), composed of black stretch pants; a big striped, hooded sweater; and a white faux-fur jacket lined in red. Little gloves of red vinyl, cork shoes, and a vinyl purse in a tartan print were the complementary accessories.

"Barbie-Q Outfit" (#962, 1959–62) included an apron with pockets big enough to hold kitchen utensils, underscoring Barbie's excellent cooking skills on top of her fashionable style.

"Peachy Fleecy Coat" (#915, 1959–61) was a soft overcoat that was just the thing for cold days in New York City.

"Cotton Casual" (#912, 1959–62) represented the classic summer sundress in blue and white stripes, whose simplicity was accentuated by two bows of white and orange ribbon on the front of the fitted bodice.

At the grand finale of every respectable fashion show is the debut of the wedding dress. "Wedding Day Set"

beaded necklace and bracelet made of silver-colored glass were furnished along with a red hatbox with Barbie's name on the lid.

The Collection of 1959

The other outfits in Barbie's wardrobe upon her debut in 1959 were narrative of the various occasions and stereotyped activities of a proper young lady in American society. The message they conveyed was of a smoothly tailored elegance, with each accessory carefully coordinated to the dress. The end result was a woman impeccably put together from every angle.

Of course, no wardrobe is complete without a delicate set of underwear for all styles of attire. For straight dresses, "Fashion Undergarments" (#919, 1959–62); for fuller

With such a complete and varied wardrobe, Barbie of course has to have a wedding dress. As the last design modeled in any well-respected fashion show even today, it embodies the dreams of multitudes of women. Barbie wears "Wedding Day Set" (1959–62) and Ken is in "Tuxedo" (1961–65).

(#972, 1959–62), made of white rayon and flowered nylon tulle and complete with the necessary bouquet and garter, lovingly portrayed the dreams and fantasies of every young girl in a fabulous white pageant.

Couture Quality

From its inception, every item in Barbie's wardrobe was labeled with a tiny cloth label that read "Barbie® © by Mattel." Generally applied to the most important component of a set, it was sewn into the back of a garment at the neck, close to the fastening, or inserted into a seam. This guaranteed quality and protected customers from innumerable knock-offs, while also adding a chic aspect to the clothes,

wherein a label guarantees status and fashionable taste.

That quality was prevalent in the tailored execution of these ensembles, which displayed close attention to detail in each individual design and resulting garment. When viewed today, the meticulous treatment of finishes— the linings, hems, zippers, and buttons, which often required work done by hand, just as they would at a real house of couture—is truly remarkable given their unusually small dimensions. The minuscule fasteners that were used on many garments were custom-made by Mattel in Japan, where a company called YKK was founded and managed by Yoshida Kogyo for the single purpose of fabricating these and other miniature accessories.

A romantic close-up of Barbie and Ken from their wedding album. This wedding remains a perennial game—continually staged but never consummated—in the quest to keep alive the fantasies of teenagers everywhere, which require Barbie to collect a variety of "useless" wedding dresses during her long, perennially youthful life.

BARBIE "WEDDING DAY" SET
(without doll) #972
Magnificent church wedding gown with formal train, fashioned for a fairy princess. Tiny mock pearl tiara holds the tiered bridal veil. White satin gown under billowing layers of flowered nylon tulle. Short white nylon gloves, sentimental blue garter, bridal bouquet and white slippers. The set, $5.00.

#972

Sketch of the "Wedding Day Set" taken from a 1960 catalog. The significance of the bridal dress is underlined by the double-page spread dedicated to it.

The Packaging

Every outfit was placed in specialized sales "paks" for the display racks of toy stores. The paks were brightly colored for easy recognition of the Barbie trademark and the names of the various dolls in the Barbie "family" who would wear the clothes. The packaging consisted mainly of flat cardboard boxes, colored on the bottom with one edge printed in stripes, so they could be stacked without wrinkling the clothes.

The various pieces of the outfit and such accessories as shoes, hat, gloves, and jewelry were sewn directly onto the bottom of the package, with the tiniest pieces bagged in cellophane or positioned under rigid transparent plastic glued to the cardboard. Everything was then placed in a cellophane envelope, tucked under and held

down by the corners of the box. A catalog that illustrated other available designs was inserted into every package as well.

For matching garments and accessory sets, the paks were simplified and reduced to pieces of cardboard encased in plastic in a way that kept the lively colors and the name, trademark, and catalog highly visible.

These ever-present catalogs were fundamental to the success and distribution of Barbie and her clothes. They were a perennial source of desire for little girls and anxiety for parents, who of course wanted to fulfill their child's wish list. By imitating the system of advertising and distribution employed by the real fashion press,

the catalogs employed a certain illustrative allure to stimulate the consumer and the collector in their young clients.

The first edition of the catalog from 1959, with a profile of Barbie over a hot-pink background on the cover, measured 4 x 5 inches and was printed in Japan in color and bound by two staples at the spine. Illustrated with high-quality, stylized graphics, it was exemplary of typical fashion sketches, showing one outfit per page accompanied by a brief description, the serial number, and the price. This style was consistent for many years.

During the 1960s, the pagination increased in accordance with the number of Barbie clothes produced, and Barbie's new friends Midge, Ken, Allan, and Skipper were pictured in various fashions on the cover. Each page then

On the facing page are a few details of tailoring: at left, the label that is sewn into every item of Barbie's wardrobe; at right, a detail of fabric printed with the Barbie logo alternating with multicolored flowers.

Left: An original accessories "pak," for "Color Coordinates" (1964–65) containing five little clutch bags made of soft vinyl in bright hues, with high heels in matching colors.

Below: The original packaging for the "Fountain Boy" outfit (1964–65), meant for Ken or Allan, is evidence of the care and detail devoted to the tiny accessories, and the attractive presentation of the sales packages.

75

displayed two designs apiece, which became increasingly detailed and pictured with greater realism. The first promotional photographs of gift packages also appeared at this time.

Barbie's formidable influence was clear from practically the moment she hit the toy market. She and her accessories were a synthesis of the fashions and attitudes of the day, a mirror of society. Created and marketed with meticulous attention to detail, Barbie's aesthetic qualities and stubborn representation of an adult universe were the basis of the success that would increase exponentially in worldwide distribution in the years to come.

Barbie

From and Fashion
1960 On

COTTON CASUAL
(without doll) #912
Sparkling navy and
white stripe cotton
play-dress.
Contrasting ribbons
accent the Empire
line. White summer
shoes. $1.00.

#912

An American woman must be able to carry a purse and an umbrella under her arm and hold onto the bus strap with the other hand. . . . She has to walk fast, though it's likely she'll be ashamed to. Exaggerated? Perhaps, but she wears dresses that are clearly made for movement, to keep up with the times, to go from one continent to another, always keeping her head about her. These dresses are made for women who drive cars, travel in planes or even jeeps, and who love to appear just a little bit spoiled and, in the evening, more than a little elegant; at times they get up at six in the morning to take unruly kids to school. These are women who know how to whip up a meal and who, even if they are not absolutely brilliant, don't make a big deal of it. (Excerpt from Polly Devlin, *Vogue 1920–1980, Moda immagine e costume*)

Facing page: Barbie, photographed inside her first house in 1962, wears the "Cotton Casual" design (1959–62).

Left: The original sketch.

While the world was entering the infamous decade of the 1960s, the world of fashion and appearances caught wind of the new aesthetic trends and morals. Always ready to translate everything into viable commercial products, it was also careful not to get dragged into critical value judgments. It was clear that many aspects of daily life were changing, seemingly with a conviction that one's well-being was equivalent to aggressive consumption.

Left: Heroine of the popular imagination, Barbie could not escape Andy Warhol's attention. He painted her in 1986. (© 1997 Andy Warhol Foundation for the Arts)

Facing page: Barbie wears "Open Road" (1961–64); a road map completes the outfit in a sketch taken from that year's catalog.

America and Europe seemed to be divided by an ocean that was more than geographic, over which they exchanged aggrandized symbols and stereotypes. In Italy, although political tumult caused the level of unemployment to climb, nothing seemed able to upset the "boom years," which culminated in 1963. The so-called economic miracle had taken a firm enough hold in the minds of Italians to transform them into more avid consumers. Two million cars were sold in the country that year, along with 1,600,000 refrigerators and 400,000 washing machines.

Across the ocean in America, the artistic world was regarded more and more as a global model that could be attained, or at least imitated. The ideas and proposals generated within its community arrived in Italy with the XXXII Venice Art Biennale, inciting an unavoidable collision with American Pop art that would elicit ferocious debates.

OPEN ROAD
(without doll) # 985 —
Barbie takes the high
fashion road with beige
sweater, striped pants, and a
car coat fastened with toggles. Her straw hat ties
with a red scarf, wedges
and real toggles match.
A map shows the way
to fun. The set, $3.50

#985

Among the changing images, youthful ones seemed
to prevail, identifying with concepts like freshness and
vitality conveyed with immediacy. It was indeed the young
who proposed a new cultural system in counterpoint to the
old mode of living that was so "Fifties." An innovative style
was becoming reality, the fruit of disparate yet converging
contributions. Tom Wolfe, a chronicler of the emerging
American culture, went looking for the roots of this style.
He concluded that the high style of the past was created by

*The 1960s saw a progression toward a
more functional adaptation of casual fashion,
one that was dynamic and sporty. Barbie's
wardrobe followed suit, not wanting to miss
the latest trend.*

"Busy Gal," a model in production between 1960 and 1961. Among the most popular professions for women in the 1960s, fashion design was one of the most sought after. Severe eyeglasses and a portfolio of sketches complete this outfit.

power and wealth; in the 1960s, however, it began to harbor "baser" inspirations from more marginalized people, instincts extracted from the everyday world of youth, from what for years had been the insignificant, ghettoized corner of art and photography, a world populated by poor kids.

An eclectic blend of new influences arrived on this wave from New York—new movements, new tendencies that assimilated and appropriated the images from the most banal, quotidian repertory by transforming them through Pop art, or through the surprises of Op art, into icons meant to depict the ephemera of recent history. The new culture did not shun kitsch or high camp influences. Artists, photographers, journalists, painters, and sculptors did not hesitate to mix with the stars of underground cinema or off-Broadway theater, while fashion and art found a happy fusion in advertising.

In this fickle America, ever eager to sweep out the "old" with little or no apprehension about starting from scratch, our Barbie maintained a solid commercial position and a successful image.

Perfectly in line, as always, with the dominant trends, Barbie had already secured her future. In 1986, Andy Warhol, the very personification of Pop art, would depict her in one of his highly celebrated portraits, thereby assuring her the enduring position of quintessential object in the collective imagination.

Fashion in the Sixties

Such a rapid diffusion of tastes and styles seems out of sync with the evolution of Barbie's wardrobe. The distribution issues and the technical modifications involved do not correlate with predictable and speedy updates synthesizing the latest trends in American and European fashion. And yet, six new outfits were added to the basic 1959 collection in 1960, followed by eight more in 1961, in addition to numerous accessories and simple coordinates. From year to year other designs were added that could also be worn by Barbie's increasing circle of friends, like Midge, who appeared in 1963. From 1967 on, the growth of the wardrobe proceeded at an even faster rate, with part of the apparel production custom-tailored to suit the taste of the destined country.

Among those who contributed to the global success of Barbie's look, we must call attention to Carol Spencer, who joined Charlotte Johnson's staff after April of 1963 in Mattel's Los Angeles creative division dedicated to fashion design. Some of today's most famous "historical" outfits carry her signature: "Black Magic Ensemble" (#1609), "Holiday Dance" (#1639), "Debutante Ball" (#1666), and many others, including the elegant intimate wear.

In particular, what emerges from a close look at this immense wardrobe was its practice of retroactive dating. At least until

#1609

BLACK MAGIC ENSEMBLE
- Magic for after-dark in the city! Black sheath dress with tulle evening cape.
- Accessories include black gloves, black shoes and a gold purse.
- (without doll) $2.00

Extremely elegant, yet essential, this evening outfit, "Black Magic Ensemble" (1964–65) carries the signature of Carol Spencer, designer since 1963 of many other significant items in Barbie's wardrobe. Inspired by sophisticated American ensembles for formal occasions, it is here worn by a "Fashion Queen" with a dark wig. The original sketch is at left.

1965–66, we could document the preservation of typical 1950s lines and tastes with extremely few concessions to the dominant fashion of the moment.

Apropos, in her article entitled "Formal Changes in High Fashion for Evening from 1959 to 1968," the fashion historian Doretta Davanzo Poli presents a concise summary of trends and attitudes. "If the Fifties were the period of burdensome garments loaded with ostentation, of overindulgence had disappeared, and the common feeling was that wealth was good and even normal. Even the buxom look, the physical trait of abundance so fashionable in the Fifties . . . faded along with padded undergarments packed with stays. In fact, a slender, much thinner feminine image came to hold sway in the popular imagination. As the symbol of youth and style, thinness became the unconditional premise of an elegance of

whimsicalities and exaggerations, of slightly ridiculous superstructures, of panels, furbelows and flounces, of draperies and of pleats that symbolized so accurately the hard-won comfort, happiness, and abundance of that period, then the Sixties were the period of a more familiar and widespread well-being that had more to do with existential security. The need to demonstrate one's riches with spectacular outward manifestations of luxury and elongated lines, lightened forms, and finally gave the body a sublime graphic stylization."

Innovations in Fashion

The 1960s were years of profound stylistic innovation in the world of fashion. In Paris in 1961, the Courrèges atelier opened, transforming the codes of high fashion by renewing the familiar repertory of line, dimension, and fabric to

SOLO IN THE SPOTLIGHT
(without doll) #982
Dramatic black glitter-gown with bare shoulders and rose corsage on nylon net flounce. Long black nylon tricot gloves. Pink scarf and bead necklace. Black plastic pumps. Plastic microphone. The set, $3.00.

#982

Facing page: Fashion with an eccentric, nonconformist flavor, a look inspired here by the colorful geometric lines of the 1960s.

This page: "Solo in the Spotlight" (1960–64). This Balenciaga design of 1951 documents the persistence of the "siren" look and style.

"Enchanted Evening" (1960–63). This sumptuous evening gown alludes to a certain French taste for asymmetrical draping that met with great success in American fashion. The resemblance between the doll and Grace Kelly is obvious in this photo from the January 16, 1956 issue of Life *magazine.*

ENCHANTED EVENING
(without doll) #983
Formal, floor-length gown with flowing train, in the elegance of pink satin. Simulated pearl necklace and drop earrings. Pink dancing pumps with silver glitter. White tricot elbow gloves. White fur stole. Complete set, $4.00.

#983

which the mass audience had become accustomed. Taking cues from the world of science fiction, a world that was thought to be in tune with an optimistic notion of progress that would guarantee an improved quality of human life, Courrèges simplified the construction of his garments to the extreme, rendering them analogous to geometric forms. No one will ever know who really invented the miniskirt—whether it was Courrèges, as the French maintain, or Mary Quant, as the English believe—but the fact remains that Courrèges shortened skirts to a sensational degree. He also introduced tight-fitting lamé evening pants, corroding

#0939

RED FLARE

Luscious red velvet ensemble. Flared coat with bell sleeves and white satin lining. Matching pillbox hat, handbag; long white gloves and red shoes. (without doll) $3.00

86
....

"Red Flare" (1962–65) with the pillbox hat made famous by Jacqueline Kennedy, seen in the photo above. Facing page, top: The "Senior Prom" (1963–64) and "Campus Sweetheart" (1965) designs; below, Ava Gardner wearing a similar evening gown.

with his innovative style the conservative habits of more traditional fashion. Even Emanuel Ungaro, who, like Courrèges, came out of the Balenciaga school of design, aimed for a style totally in sync with the new feminine image of the times: "I want women's skirts so short they'll seduce the whole world."

In 1962, the house of Yves Saint Laurent opened in Paris, launching the designer's new and curious designs that contrasted with the dominant traditionalism. Among his many collections, we remember the one in 1965 that utilized motifs taken from the paintings of Mondrian, evoking a coldly geometric and essential linearity. In 1966 his shows became famous for clothes that were clearly inspired by Pop art and Andy Warhol. Among the many standout figures who helped create the global image of fashion in the 1960s, we remember the Italian designers Pucci, who with his intensely colored pantsuits became a commercial phenomenon capable of unifying practicality

#0954

CAREER GIRL
Classic two-piece tweed suit, with red sleeveless shell. Hat matches suit, sparked with red rose. Black elbow length gloves and black pumps. (without doll) $3.00

88

Ken wears "Business Appointment" (1966–67), and Barbie is in "Career Girl" (1963–64). The names of the two designs suggest a certain work-oriented lifestyle, for which the elegance of the 1960s serves as the best calling card.

and elegance; and Valentino, who, in those years, became the most celebrated dressmaker in Italian couture, consecrated as such by a rich and eccentric international clientele, including Farah Diba and Jacqueline Kennedy.

The Influence of the Film World

Under the influence of this impassioned tumble of innovation, the outfits that took shape to enrich Barbie's wardrobe nevertheless wanted to keep control of the situation by addressing taste and tailoring with a prescribed, formal severity that was clearly independent of more flamboyant fashions. The most interesting, novel contribution came from the world of American movie costumers who, by dressing the stars with no distinction between on-screen and social occasions, happily promoted high glamour. By

Below: A detail of the elegant purse of gold-plated cardboard trimmed in the same faux fur as the garment at right.

The "Saturday Matinee" ensemble (1965) represents one of the most elegant and, consequently, successful suits in Barbie's wardrobe. The fine woven tweed with golden and polychrome threads, the tailored lines, the large fitted collar, and the faux fur trim make this a work of haute couture in miniature.

89

The "Barbie Fashion Shop" (1963) is the new atelier for Barbie and her friends. Constructed in re-closeable cardboard, it is transported and assembled with ease. The two dolls are wearing "After Five" (1962–64), a black-and-white piece inspired by Dior, seen in the original sketch below, and a modern replica of "Senior Prom."

91

#0934

AFTER FIVE

Princess-style dress of black faille with portrait collar of white organdy, button accent on bodice. Organdy picture hat with black velvet bow and black shoes. (without doll) $2.00

*"Theatre Date"
(1963) is a uniquely
elegant dress in
emerald-green satin,
complete with a
pillbox hat. The
close-fitting straight
skirt is overlaid with
a peplum gathered at
the waist. The short
bolero jacket with
wide shawl collar is
presented a second
time, together with
the hat, in the "Satin
Bolero" pak of the
same year in varied
colors: white, black,
hot pink, and pastel
pink with sequins.*

92

*In Barbie's wardobe, line,
color, and materials are combined with often curious results,
and yet it always remains on
the threshold of elegance.*

abandoning the precise dictates of European fashion disseminated in the pages of *Vogue*, they created a world where the evocative innuendo and the exaltation of a character got the better of haute couture. Certain Barbie doll outfits debuted in those years that reflected this vivid Hollywood appetite.

"Solo in the Spotlight" (#982, 1960–64) perfectly illustrated this notion of combining dress and costume. Made of a black stretch fabric, the strapless dress was fitted down to the calf and flared at the bottom in the typical "siren" line with a flounce of tulle accented by a dramatic pink fabric rose. Long black gloves; high heels; a multi-strand necklace of silver-colored glass beads; a large pink handkerchief to hold in the hand; and a standing microphone completed and defined the overall image. Evocative of the smoky atmosphere of the elegant nightclubs so dear to American cinematography, where the blond, defenseless singer is always rescued from the gangster's advances by the helpful detective, "Solo in the Spotlight" is a classic that will endure in its portrayal of a certain kind of glamorous woman.

Who better than Marilyn Monroe to comment on such a dress? From the aforementioned interview (see p. 47): "I bought my first evening dress for the annual dinner of the Foreign Press Association, where I received the Henrietta award and was presented as one of the most promising young actresses in Hollywood. I was very happy to get the award . . . but I know that some of the women there thought that my dress was a little too much for the occasion. I considered their opinions but concluded that their reasons were not good enough to make me take the dress back to Oleg Cassini, who designed it. I have always admired his taste and his imagination in women's clothes and my dress was a confirmation of this. It was designed in red velvet, hugging the body all over to the knee and then inverted to the floor in the style of Lillian Russell. It's a little tight in front but not too much. Frankly, I adore this dress and I would like to have more occasions to wear it." A very memorable image from the October 1950 French *Vogue* showed the model Lisa Fonssagrives, splendidly photographed by Irving Penn, wearing an altogether similar design by Marcel Rochas.

Another fabulous outfit was "Enchanted Evening" (#983, 1960–63). With its luxurious elegance, it could have been conceived to celebrate the legendary Academy Awards ceremony.

Left: "On the Avenue" (1965), a truly exceptional design in the cut of the jacket, choice of fabric, and coordinated accessories.

Right: "Matinee Fashion" (1965), chiffon and leopard combined for daytime elegance. *Below:* "Benefit Performance" (1966–67), with tulle and red velvet for society benefits.

93

The quintessence of femininity and proverbial stardom, the whole dress is made of pale pink satin, with a fitted bodice that bares the shoulders. The close-fitting skirt, tighter at the calf, is composed of abundant fabric gathered on the left side to form a very dramatic drape over the legs, which then cascades down the back to form an ample train—all to great theatrical effect. The accessories are equally stylish: a pearl necklace in three strands with a pendant at the clasp; transparent heels speckled with gold; and, as a final touch, a stole of white rabbit fur lined in the same pink satin as the dress. The sources of inspiration for this design are many, though clearly closer to the fashion of the early 1950s than that of the '60s. Indeed, A. Glenn

Mandeville, in his *Doll Fashion Anthology and Price Guide*, cites an interesting precedent in this regard, referencing the Castillo design photographed on the cover of American *Vogue* back in 1949.

Jackie's Style

At the beginning of the 1960s, Americans were enraptured by a new public figure destined for legendary status, Jacqueline Bouvier Kennedy. A tangible persona, not an artificial product of Hollywood's star factory, she evoked in the popular imagination—and not just in America—the essence of class, elegance, and sophistication. It would take the journalistic indiscretions that followed her second —and much maligned—marriage to the wealthy Greek shipping magnate Aristotle Onassis to drive home the full extent of her endless wardrobe and the millions of dollars spent keeping it up to date. Among her favorite European designers, Balenciaga supplied the former First Lady with dresses and accessories that were appropriate to her image, and managed to use the international fame of this exceptional model to obtain the perfect fusion between his sartorial style and her strong personality. Among the most heralded images of the epoch was the infamous "pillbox" hat worn with the very stylish A-line overcoats and dresses.

These clearly meaningful elements were the ones found in the "Red Flare" design (#939, 1962–65), which consists of a flaming-red coat and the inevitable pillbox hat. The references to Balenciaga were clear. Beyond the celebrated hat, we find the great designer's imprimatur in the strongly flared line; in the bell-shaped sleeves characterized by a dropped shoulder seam; and in the

tiny flat bows that decorate the rolled collar at the clasp and at the back of the hat. Made of cotton velveteen, it is lined in white satin, closed by a hidden button, and finished with an envelope-shaped clutch also in velvet and lined in white; the required long white gloves; and the traditional red high heels. Another echo of Dior's "New Look" was found in the formal "Senior Prom" (#951, 1963–64), all tulle and softness in its clarion call to the allure of the great romantic ball. It displayed a shimmering aura with its form-fitting, strapless bodice and full skirt in emerald-green satin covered with separate panels of alternating blue and green net tulle gathered at the waist, creating dazzling effects with the transparent layering of colors. The green high heels decorated with a tiny pearl made the outfit more precious.

The continuing popularity of the "New Look" was confirmed by another formal ensemble that repeated the pattern in a different color: "Campus Sweetheart" (#1616, 1965) was a dress in white satin with pink and red tulle panels.

While skirts continued to get shorter in 1965, and tailored construction tended to loosen form and volume, the collection created for Barbie that year persisted with a precise, formal rigor.

Facing page, above: "Sophisticated Lady" (1963–64), a dress for formal evenings out; below, "Magnificence" (1965), yet another example of red as the preferred color of true elegance. Right: The "Fashion Luncheon" suit (1966–67) and, in the "mod" style, the "Fashion Shiner" outfit (1967–68); two different interpretations of fashion that are both traditional and up-to-the-minute.

From left: Francie wears "Clear Out" (1967); Black Francie with the "Denims On!" outfit (1967); Stacey in "All That Jazz" (1968); Casey with the "Orange Zip" design (1968), very similar to the one by Mary Quant on the facing page. Finally, Francie, with the "Culotte Wot" ensemble (1968), characterized by the eccentric sunglasses. At right, a few accessories sold with Francie's wardrobe.

Along these lines, three elegant suits became very significant: "Saturday Matinee" (#1615), "On the Avenue" (#1644), and "Gold 'N Glamour" (#1647). Made with great display of haute couture elements—precise cut, detailed construction, and coordinated accessories—they were tailored in expensive fabrics woven with gold threads and garnished with borders of dyed fake fur. The cut of the dresses adhered to the body and was designed to show off the figure, though the hem of the skirt stayed below the knee. Haute couture details were incorporated into the jackets: the big, fitted collar of "Saturday Matinee;" the coordinated scarf in "Gold 'N Glamour;" and the stylish, gold-plated demi-belt in "On the Avenue," which only cinched the fullness of the fabric in front, that otherwise fell freely in the back.

The Unsurpassed Style of Dior

The imprint of the House of Dior, which opened a wholesale ready-to-wear boutique in New York in 1949, was again very evident in these items, both in the technique and elegant conception. The style was so widespread in the American aesthetic that it remained a continual source of inspiration for domestic designers. In the October 15, 1962 issue of American *Vogue* was a John Weitz design photographed by Bruce Davidson that displayed obvious structural affinities with "On the Avenue."

The timeless classicism of Chanel was revisited in the "Fashion Luncheon" suit (#1656, 1966–67). It was among the most sophisticated designs in Barbie's wardrobe. In traditional pink, its design and cut were original, simple, and impeccable, especially in the short jacket that was open in the front with a curved asymmetrical hem and bordered by a high-rolled collar

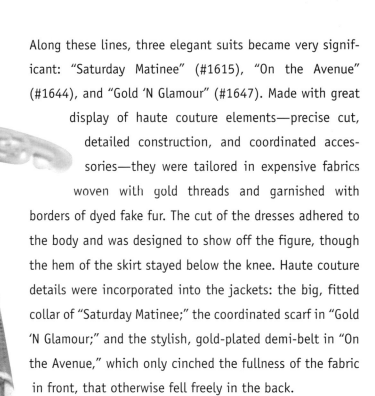

in colored satin. The one-piece dress underneath had a satin sleeveless bodice in a fabric that, like that of the jacket, imitates the weave of linen. The colored hat, long white gloves, and high-heeled pumps were the essential accessories.

The Arrival of 1968

The last years of the 1960s bore testimony to historic events that would profoundly change opinions and mentalities to those now taken for granted. The younger generation's sense of renewal and the continual need to experiment, coupled with a growing desire to establish a better, more enlightened rapport with the self and nature, carried Western society toward a generational conflict that was increasingly violent. A sense of incomprehension dominated relations between parents and children, which led to the historical labeling of an entire generation as "rebels" and "hippies." An abyss seemed to open between the two worlds, an open generational conflict in which order and conservatism were pitted against a desire for freedom and innovation. These positions were not always maintained with clarity; history now permits us to examine those events at an objective distance. It remains clear that so much malaise was certain to provoke violence.

Nineteen-sixty-eight was the year of the

big strikes and protests that saw students and workers joined together for the first time. Working side by side, the student demonstrations invested the union protests with intellectualism.

In the United States, where the escalation of the Vietnam War became a national tragedy and a yet unresolved issue, Martin Luther King and Robert Kennedy were assassinated. Meanwhile, the press and the media showed us the Soviet invasion of Prague and the horrors of famine in Biafra, dealing a hard blow to the illusory sense of our own well-being.

At the same time, England's cultural influence on the United States became more widespread, as the British invasion spread from London, a capital in creative ferment, across all of Europe, and finally landed on America's shores. Millions of young people dreamed of love and peace and let their hair grow to the music of the Beatles. The musical *Hair* debuted on Broadway and consecrated as a cultural phenomenon the ideology of the "flower children," whose motto, "make love, not war," definitively separated the factions of the politically engaged from those who felt indifference and practiced sexual freedom.

The fashion establishment attempted to establish rules within a world that no longer had any, where anything could happen and be reinvented. At La Scala opera house in Milan,

on the occasion of the legendary premiere of *Don Carlos* on December 7, 1968, tomatoes tossed by students at the women's glamorous evening attire dictated the end of a time lived under the rubric of manners and etiquette. The great creators of fashion would continue to work discreetly for a highly exclusive international clientele, in a seemingly lethargic period leading up to the grand reawakening of the 1980s.

The new female archetypes bore the faces of models Veruschka, Marisa Berenson, Twiggy, and Jean Shrimpton. The beauty ideal exalted intense gazes, eyes enlarged by somewhat oriental makeup, and full lips tinted in soft pearlized colors. Long legs reigned supreme on youthful, thin bodies that were almost androgynous and were adorned with short, colorful dresses fabricated in everything from plastic to metal.

Barbie wears the
"Jump into Lace"
design (1968). The
wearing of pantsuits
even for formal
occasions is by now an
approved practice, as
evidenced by Emilio
Pucci's similar design
photographed below.

The "New" Barbie

Barbie changed her features, too, with a new face and makeup designs that were more in tune with contemporary tastes. Her wardrobe was renewed by the introduction of emphatically "mod" outfits that seemed to have just flown through the doors of London's Carnaby Street boutiques.

The aforementioned classical and elegant dresses seemed very far away at this point, some remaining in distribution for just a few years. The new collection brought about the first clean break with the past, aligning Barbie more definitively with contemporary fashion. Even the names seemed more essential, expressing concepts and manners that were considered up to date. "Sunflower" (#1683, 1967–68) was a short, straight, sleeveless little dress with a scooped neck, whose vivid floral print covered the entire front of the dress. The big round pendant earrings in shocking pink and blue plastic were a clear sign of the very latest in fashion—new, lightweight, and intensely colored materials.

"Print Aplenty" (#1686, 1967–68) was also inspired by mod designs, attracted to them by the contrast of geometric and naturalistic motifs. With a cut similar to "Sunflower," this one displayed a lively colored print resembling small bricks. Here again, the geometric earrings in hot-pink plastic were matched by the color of the high-heeled pumps.

The prevalence of pants in women's fashion was by now confirmed. Limited a few years earlier to sportswear or daywear, pants soon became an established part of formal evening apparel as well. Motivated by a presumed equality between the sexes, pants

Francie, Barbie's cousin, made her market debut in 1966. With this lively "Gad-About" suit from the same year, her look implies a decisive break with the more traditional elegance that was promoted earlier in Barbie's wardrobe. The "mod"

101

explosion was based on the new London fashion trend, whose creative roots were found in the boutiques of the youthful Carnaby Street.

no longer remained hidden under long outer garments, but instead were exposed in their totality, rejecting the convention that projected elegant women exclusively in dresses and long skirts. Irene Galitzine created a costume phenomenon—considered scandalous in proper society—with the pantsuits she called "palazzo pajamas." Presented at her first show in Rome's Pitti Palace in 1960, these truly novel garments were a huge success, convincing even the most traditional women to wear them. "Caribbean Cruise" (#1687, 1967) was a charming yellow "palazzo" pantsuit with a low, square-cut top and wide pants trimmed with nylon ruffles, a perfect interpretation of this style. "Patio Party" (#1692, 1967–68) posed the same theme. In perfect synchronicity with fashion of the time, it coupled a "palazzo pajama" in a brightly colored print jersey with a bi-color, green-and-blue satin tunic marked by a deep vent in front. Conspicuous round earrings and blue high heels completed the ensemble.

New dolls also joined the Barbie family in these years, some of whom were significant in their close relationship to the world of fashion, by which they were directly inspired.

Francie arrived in 1966 and was introduced as one of Barbie's cousins. The features and the physical struc-

Twiggy was undoubt-edly one of the most famous models of the 1960s. In the photo above is her doll incarnation wearing the "Twiggy Gear" *(1968) outfit. Facing page: "Live Action Barbie" (1971) dons the fringes and colors of hippie fashion.*

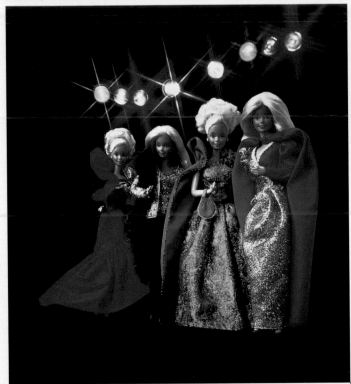

type of woman. Presented as "London's Top Teen Model," she was the first Mattel doll copied precisely from real life, and she was cut from the same mold so she could wear all the other dolls' clothes. At this point Barbie was the undisputed top model in production, whose success surpassed by a long shot those of the most celebrated real-life models. She approached the 1970s amidst ear-shattering rock and disco music and surrounded by a wide group of relatives and friends whose diverse nationalities and races are united by one great passion: clothes.

The Practical Seventies

The 1970s saw America's attention shift to a harsher reality and attitude toward daily life. During the first three months of 1971, there was a national recession in the United States

ture of this new character took on a more adolescent image—tall and slender—while the distinctly mod wardrobe contrasted with the refined and classically elegant one previously worn by Barbie. Materials introduced by young London designers of Carnaby Street—including brilliantly colored plastics; glossy transparent vinyls printed with vivid colors; print jerseys with contrasting motifs; glittering lamés; cotton and nylon prints in a vast array of dots, stripes, flowers, and checks—were put to perfect use in these tiny outfits. Another new doll entered the market in 1967 as an American friend of Francie. Casey's body used the same mold as Francie, so she could wear the same full wardrobe, but she was differentiated by her smiling face and short hair styled to the latest fashion. Twiggy was yet another doll to appear that year, an exact replica of the famous model of the same name who, with her exceptionally thin figure, helped call attention to a new

inspired by the famous prints of the Florentine designer Emilio Pucci.

Left: "Fashion Jeans Barbie" (1982); simplicity and novelty are synthesized in this interpretation of the most popular article of clothing in the world.

Facing page, above: Some shimmering designs from Oscar de la Renta's 1985 collection in pure

Hollywood style; below, "Totally Hair Barbie" (1992), one of the most widely sold dolls, in a minidress

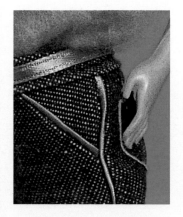

that would cripple the economy, striking the world of fashion as well. The free spending of the 1960s disappeared, swept away by the new economic contingencies.

Intent on recapturing practicality, the world of high fashion renounced its gratuitous exhibitionism. A hierarchical system began to emerge, aimed at categorizing social groups and types that could be differentiated by distinct styles of clothing. However, among the ever more intense generational conflicts, the "message" of fashion would dissolve in the face of youthful spontaneity, as young people began to rebel against prefabricated products. Their new "uniform" consisted of a pair of blue jeans, a garment that would steadily gain influence, unifying cultures and races all over the planet under a standard image.

Mattel faced a difficult year in 1970 with one of its first big disasters. A fire broke out in the Mexican factory that had become so important in production after the closing of the Japanese plant. This was also the year of Michelangelo Antonioni's famous film *Zabriskie Point*, in which he blew up a metaphorical "villa of luxury and consumerism" in an extraordinary sequence repeated in slow motion that was emblematic of the profound crisis in which the system found itself. But the great consumer machine could not be stopped. While fashionable young people dressed in gaudy psychedelic colors and fringe and bell-bottom jeans covered with multicolored patches, rediscovering a taste for casual, fun clothing, Barbie and her friends continued to entertain their juvenile public, perfectly decked out in new outfits like "Live Action" of 1971, that came complete with microphone and record album. The continual evolution of Barbie's image seemed to fear no obstacles, be they historical or societal. With an alchemist's facility, Mattel reinterpreted world events and used them to its advantage. Incorporating the company's wealth of experience and Barbie's vast notoriety, Mattel consistently concentrated its effort on the final product, achieving incredible results.

A Record-Setting Doll

Since 1959 more than one billion Barbie dolls and related friends have been produced. Lined up head to toe, they would form a chain that could circle the earth more than eleven times. More than 115 million yards of fabric have been used to manufacture clothes for the Barbie clan, with about 120 new outfits created every year. Barbie also maintains a huge passion for animals, with few apparent limitations on size and characteristics. She currently owns 17 dogs, 11 horses, 5 cats, a parrot, a chimpanzee, a panda, a lion cub, a giraffe, a zebra, a dolphin, and a whale. These astonishing and entertaining facts help us better understand the import of this stupefying commercial phenomenon and, even more, the import of fashion. During the 1980s, the development of Barbie's wardrobe involved

Facing page: Barbie wears "Benefit Ball," a fabulous evening gown in gold and marbled-blue lamé, designed specifically by Carol Spencer in 1992 to launch the "Classique" series. The doll's hairdo and makeup were styled expressly for this design.

Below: Another opulent dress for formal evenings designed for Barbie by Bill Blass in 1997.

a variety of styles and trends. Among the most significant is the collection "Astro Fashion," designed in 1985 by Carol Spencer and inspired by the world of science fiction; and a design done in the same year by Oscar de la Renta based on evening gowns in brilliant colors of lamé. These were two opposing worlds, yet both embodied emblematic aspects of this doll's power to charm. Her image could make a smooth transition from the latest galactic fantasy to the flashy and somewhat free-spirited atmosphere of a California television series.

In 1985, Barbie achieved her ultimate "consecration" within the world of adult fashion thanks to the energetic creativity of the French designer Billy Boy. He revived the "fashion as theater" concept and adapted it perfectly to the international image of Barbie. He based his concept on the exhibition "Le Petit Théâtre de la Mode," which was introduced in April of 1945 at the Musée des Arts Décoratifs in Paris, and toured the major European capitals, New York City, and San Francisco in an effort to publicize and garner appreciation for Parisian fashion. This

Luxury, sophistication, and charm, lavished without restraint on these spectacular designs worn by Barbie, are the elements to which Mattel remains steadfastly dedicated, especially in light of the success of the limited edition dolls for collectors. Here, with the "Billions of Dreams" doll from 1997, fashion is only a pretext for evoking a dreamlike vision that is the apotheosis of a timeless aesthetic.

In the "Designer" series, Barbie is dressed by the world's best-known designers. At left we see her in a sports outfit by Calvin Klein from 1996. On the facing page, she models a glamorous embroidered evening dress designed in 1995 by Ferré for Dior.

post–World War II initiative sought to revitalize the French fashion community and to restore its prewar supremacy.

As was traditional in France, where the relationship between the pure and applied arts has always been close, many artisans collaborated to create "Le Petit Théâtre de la Mode," intended to display the styles of contemporary fashion in miniature. Fifty-three Parisian dressmakers, 37 milliners, 21 hairdressers, and roughly 20 accessory production houses worked together to dress tiny mannequins, made at one-quarter life size, that were destined to spread the "New Look." Billy Boy's modern concept was not so rigidly nationalistic; rather, he sought to engage both European and American designers as well, who were all invited to dress Barbie, his exceptional model. "The New Theater of Fashion" thus debuted with a great retinue of prestigious designer labels who, by way of this brilliant compilation of costume and publicity supported by Mattel, aided in raising the allure of Barbie to a legendary height.

The Collectors' Barbie

In 1986 a series of porcelain Barbie dolls was introduced. It was a limited edition series of dolls intended for an adult audience who, with a pang of nostalgia, had recently rediscovered Barbie as a collectible phenomenon. The first model in this series was "Blue Rhapsody," which was followed by others that reintroduced some of Barbie's most famous attire produced between 1959 and 1967. In celebration of the Barbie doll's thirtieth birthday in 1989, 38 of the most famous French fashion designers paid her homage by creating exclusive designs just for her; twelve of the most renowned French hair stylists then attended to her hair. In honor of this occasion, Mattel produced these dolls using kanekalon for their hair, a new, easy-to-comb fiber that could hold a hairstyle for a much longer period of time.

Representative of expert, "made in USA" stylistic practices, the dolls became part of another new product line based on quality materials and finishes. The first, from 1992, called "Benefit Ball Barbie," was designed by Carol Spencer, with Mellie Phillips styling the elaborate hair and Hiroe Okubo-Wolf doing the facial makeup. The sumptuous evening dress in blue-and-gold lamé was accentuated by the shimmering iridescence of the fabric that, with its complex, tailored construction, reintroduced the glamour that characterized American fashion in the 1960s.

To accentuate her connection to contemporary international fashion in the 1990s, the "Designer" series inaugurated a new collection in which Barbie wore dresses by famous designers like Nicole Miller ("Savvy Shopper," 1994), Christian Dior (1995), Donna Karan (1995), Escada (1996), and Calvin Klein (1996).

These were only a few of the market initiatives that Mattel pursued between the late 1980s and '90s in its continuing effort to focus on the symbiosis of Barbie and fashion. Despite the tremendous variety of information that designers and the fashion industry have presented to a confused, yet eager public at an increasingly urgent pace, Barbie has kept her head admirably, testing every possible vocabulary—from the nostalgic pursuit of haute couture to modern cinematographic and professional imagery, from domestic ready-to-wear to colorful ethnic costumes. Her true loyalty, however, is to that boundless army of little girls who, from the day she first appeared, have found in her the key to the great game of life: dreams and the world of make-believe—amidst little pink houses, elegant dresses, profusely outfitted campers, and perennially tan boyfriends—can secure a future of serenity, where being carefree is the first rule of life. We may conclude by citing Quentin Bell, the fashion historian: "Fashion, for those who live under its reign, is an irresistible force of incalculable importance. Overwhelming, at times pitiless, it governs our behavior, conditions our sexual appetites, colors our erotic imagination, at once renders all things possible, but also distorts the meaning we are able to find in history, and determines our aesthetic criteria."

111

Barbie

Professions and Pomp in the Mirror

There are no rules to the game. It is a subtle, repetitive mimicry, a preparation for the world beyond the looking-glass. (Carl Fox, *The Doll*)

One thing is clear: Barbie does not fear contradictions. Quite the contrary. She thrives

Facing page: Barbie wearing the "Sissi" costume (1996). Left: The 1865 portrait of the Empress Elizabeth of Austria by F. X. Winterhalter.

113

on them. They are the essence of her being, permitting the seemingly infinite perpetuation of her legend. As strident as the color of her clothes—like the shocking pink that has become the symbol of her protected universe—these conflicts define this chameleon-like doll, who so readily transforms herself from a tender, fresh-faced schoolteacher into a fabulous movie star dripping with sequins. The unclothed Barbie is disarming and does not invite such fervid meditations; she declares her nature simply, as a doll/mannequin, and displays her vinyl joints with no false modesty. When exposed, the very stuff she is made of seems miserly and not very intriguing. It is her serial nature, the fact that she is one in an endless army of clones, that strips her of existential possibility, until the magic moment when she dons one outfit out of a million possible choices. With those few inches of colored cloth slipped over her "skin," her status as international icon is once again rendered recognizable.

Never was the fate of a toy more stressful! To exist as a shell that must continually refashion itself in order to render itself desirable and, above all, saleable.

How to carry on, then, after having tested all the possible styles that fashion has invented, after trying on the newest colors and fabrics, after wearing designer labels from all over the world? Wherein lies the element of surprise? Conflicts and contradictions: Barbie does not have enough history to fear them. It is profoundly mistaken to accuse Barbie, as some have, of inducing premature desires in budding little consumers. The scholar Carla Rocchi, cited earlier, feels that to focus attention on

a grown-up doll by positively emphasizing her tastes and consumer preferences is to predetermine a child's future inclinations in an abusive way; it could be said, if the paradigm were not excessive, that Barbie acts as a kind of pusher to create addictions through forcefully induced needs.

In response to this criticism, one could offer that Barbie represents everything that can be represented simply because she exists as a vehicle for a child's own fertile imagination. She does not lead into temptation; she is not the adult vehicle of consumerism, the devil in a blond wig. She is only that which she is asked to be—and this at the risk of being resigned to the garbage can and rapidly replaced with some other doll or toy that is more current. The writer Luca Goldoni took Barbie's side in an article entitled *Barbie non suscita pensieri peccaminosi* [*Barbie Does Not Stir Up Sinful Thoughts*], published on January 8, 1996 in the Italian journal *Corriere della Sera*. "Children notoriously fantasize while they play," she wrote. "They act. They want to become that which they are not. They pretend to be mothers, plumbers, doctors, and teachers, and they're not happy if they have to be the kids or the students. Once we establish that they have a right to these fantasies . . . the richer the fantasy, the more fun they have . . . . But I don't believe that any child of normal parents actually dreams of one day having a pink camper or a horse with a platinum blond mane. The little girls who play with Barbie dolls are not blinded to their live reality, just as their mothers are not, even though they do the ironing while escaping into television soap operas. Italian mothers grew up with sumptuous Lenci dolls that wore makeup like the stars of silent movies. But they continued to do the laundry for the rest of their lives." In these so-called modern times, when we are told that technological advances will solve our problems,

#991
REGISTERED NURSE
(without doll) #991
Barbie cures patients in a trim white cotton uniform with zipper back, buttoned blouse and real hip pockets. With her spectacles and graduate nurse's cap, she wears a navy blue cape lined in red silk for outside calls. Hot water bottle, diploma, medicine bottle and spoon complete the set. $3.00.

Facing page: A scene from the daily life of the Barbie doll clan (the convertible car was produced by the Irwin Corporation).

Left: The "Registered Nurse" outfit (1961–64). The most "realistic" professions of the time were often used to create easily recognizable personas within the multifaceted universe of Barbie. Above, the original catalog sketch.

the most disparate messages fill every moment of daily life and expectations are piled high, giving voice to the wishes and needs of others. So, is Barbie going to be any more "coercive" if she has a cellular phone, a fitness program, a year-round tan, access to the Internet, lottery tickets, long vacations, holiday treats, etc.? All Barbie does is put us in the scene—the pre-existing adult world—along with all the manias and conventions that have become a part of our daily lives. In the "little theater" in which she is the prima donna, she storms through a bevy of roles and attitudes, and manages—thanks to the great looking-glass of childhood play—to show us how we really are.

Beyond the formal clothing that forms the foundation of Barbie's wardrobe—one which is consonant with and reassuring for the woman whose femininity corresponds to easily recognizable, precise canons—we find garments that were intentionally created to represent the most diverse and curious professions and social functions.

A New Professional Look

Despite contradictions, the female role in American society has always carried a determinate weight, generating over the years its own rich, though turbulent, history. Thus, we were not surprised in 1965, when Mattel, in a decidedly avant-garde move, put the "Miss Astronaut" (#1641) outfit on the market. In it, Barbie became a quintessential astronaut, adopting the same type of spacesuit used by NASA. Twenty years before a woman was sent into space, Barbie wore her clothes. Not bad for a doll!

In the preceding years, Barbie's official "career" had followed more or less the same steps as the entry of real women into the workplace. In 1961 Barbie donned the "American Airlines Stewardess" (#984) ensemble and acted out a career that many girls wanted, one that was well paid

Allan and Barbie wear, respectively, "Mr. Astronaut" and "Miss Astronaut" from 1965. The two spacesuits are not complete without a tiny American flag, testimony to the first manned space orbit.

and guaranteed a life of freedom and discovery in countless journeys around the world.

The work life of this particular profession fascinated girls with pretty faces, seemingly the fundamental requirement for being hired. It promised a dynamic future guaranteed by jet-age technological advances, which shortened time and distance. Based on these and other types of advances, the social role of women experienced another push toward the notions of freedom and equality. Many American women began to live alone by choice in their quest for autonomy, supporting themselves with their own jobs before getting married, convinced that they would thereby achieve that parity with men and begin to break down the time-honored rituals of dependency. It would take the 1980s and '90s to demonstrate how distant the fruition of this autonomy could be from the old feminist ideal. For that dearly bought independence often meant something quite different: hard work inside a man's

#984

AMERICAN AIRLINES STEWARDESS

(without doll) #984
Barbie takes off for sky adventures in her flight blue uniform with flight insignia on cap and jacket. Her white nylon blouse and shoulder pocketbook are trimly tailored to regulations. An American Airlines flight bag travels with her. The set, $3.50.

Barbie's wardrobe reflects one of the most popular women's careers of the 1960s, as she is seen here wearing the "American Airlines Stewardess" outfit (1961–64). As illustrated in the original catalog sketch, the ensemble comes complete with all the necessary accessories.

world that, especially to women on their own, concedes nothing with ease.

On the other end of the spectrum, the ethereal image of the classical ballerina suggests many a young girl's hopes for the beauty, grace, and discreet femininity that, especially during the 1960s and '70s, seemed to be the highest aspiration of the female middle class. The

Sketch of the outfit "Ballerina" (1961–65), in which various dancing accessories are also pictured and described.

proliferation of dance schools and the large number of little girls obliged by stern mothers and dedicated teachers to slip on those uncomfortable toe shoes testified to the artistic power of this vision, for some children an often very materialistic one. "Ballerina" (#989), the outfit created by Mattel in 1961 and produced until 1965, was perfectly aligned with this tendency. It outfitted Barbie in a classical tutu with traditional black tights for her dance classes; among the various accessories was the playbill from Tchaikovsky's *Nutcracker* ballet, in which our doll naturally interpreted the role of the Sugar Plum Fairy.

Between these extremes, the "Registered Nurse" ensemble (#991, 1961–64) seemed to suggest a much more

BALLERINA
(without doll) #989
Barbie dances before kings and queens as the Sugar Plum Fairy, costumed in a shimmering silver tutu. A program announces her performance. For practice at the barre, she wears a black jersey leotard and tights. Pink satin shoe bag holds her ballet slippers. The set. $3.00

realistic profession. Dressed as a nurse and accessorized with a diploma, severe eyeglasses with black frames, medicines, and a hot water bag, Barbie found herself in one of the most traditional female roles, whose star quality is extreme patience. In a design more in tune with the everyday life of many young students intent on rounding out their weekly wages, the "Barbie Babysits" (#953, 1963–64) outfit engaged our doll in the more tranquil role of babysitter, furnished with the various necessary objects for the serious nature of this work, including a list of emergency phone numbers (doctor, fire department, police); a telephone; and, of course, a baby bottle to keep the baby contented. In addition, glasses, books, an alarm clock, and a box of saltines served to pass the time while Barbie waited for the parents to return.

"Student Teacher" (#1622, 1965–66) engaged Barbie in a geography lesson with a world globe, a book, and a pointer. The red fitted dress with matching high heels caused a few doubts about the seriousness of this teacher, while leaving none regarding her charm. These were a few of the typical early professions to which Barbie was directed, professions that would be repeated in the years to come. Though updated and modified, they were essentially faithful to the original motivations.

If these roles of nurse, babysitter, and teacher were

Barbie wears "Student Teacher" (1965–66); original sketch and details of the accessories.

119

Barbie's Professions*

1959	Teenage Fashion Model
1961	Ballerina, Registered Nurse, American Airlines Stewardess
1963	Graduate, Career Girl
1964	Candy Striper Volunteer
1965	Astronaut, Fashion Editor, Student Teacher
1966	Pan Am Stewardess
1973	Surgeon
1975	Olympic Athlete: Downhill Skier, Figure Skater, Gymnast
1984	Aerobics Instructor
1985	Business Executive, Dress Designer, TV News Reporter, Veterinarian, Teacher
1986	Astronaut, Rock Star
1988	Doctor
1989	UNICEF Ambassador, Doctor, Army Officer, Dancer on a TV Dance Club Show
1990	U.S. Air Force Pilot, Summit Diplomat, Ice Capades Star, Rock Star
1991	Music Video Star, Naval Petty Officer
1992	Marine Corps Sergeant, Rap Musician, Rollerblade® In-line Skater, Teacher, Chef, Business Woman, Doctor, Presidential Candidate
1993	Police Officer, Army Medic, Radio City Music Hall Rockette, Baseball Player
1994	Pediatrician, Astronaut, Scuba Diver, Air Force Thunderbird Squadron Leader, Artist
1995	Teacher, Lifeguard, Firefighter
1996	Teacher, Pet Doctor, Engineer, Olympic Gymnast
1997	Dentist, Paleontologist, Boutique owner

*Listed by the name used for international distribution

considered morally sound, it was because they were based on the historic female model as nurturer, and therefore appeared reassuring to the eyes of adults who envisioned their little girls quietly at play and safely removed from any desire to be either a disco dancer or, worse, a supermodel. There were many other anxieties in store for parents of Barbie lovers however, as is evident from the list of professions ventured by this dynamic doll from 1959 to 1994. In 1985, when "career women" burst onto the scene, Barbie lost no time and immediately aligned herself with the new wave of yuppie blonds wearing designer Armani suits. There she was as a manager and as a television reporter, perfectly assimilating the roles that placed her on the cutting-edge career tracks. Barbie moved beyond, but did not forget, the domestic attitudes that she had promoted until that time.

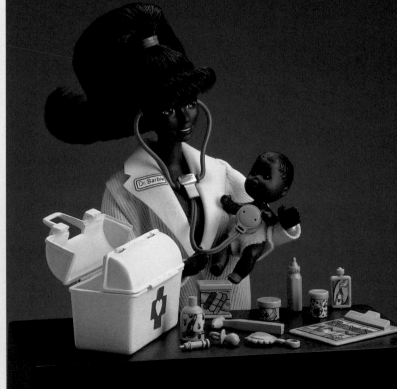

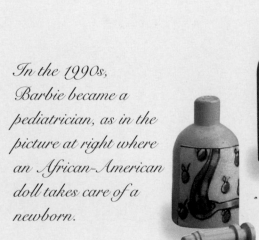

In the 1990s, Barbie became a pediatrician, as in the picture at right where an African-American doll takes care of a newborn.

Among the many points of departure in the roles invented for Barbie, here she is in the prestigious, however incredible, version "Barbie for President" (1992), produced in a special edition for the toy store Toys 'R' Us. The packaging also includes a red velvet suit, various accessories, and the compulsory electoral badge.

In that year began a new period of conflict in which Barbie was projected into a stream of "realities" and behavioral models that were totally different one from another.

In a time increasingly dominated by the mass media and its amplification of everyday events, the concept of individual identity was more quickly dissolved in the face of ubiquitous, powerful advertising and the growing uncertainty about an all too close and foreseeable future. Through all this, the only rational image, smiling in every role that was imposed upon her, was Barbie with her synthetic face and everlasting composure.

Barbie in Hollywood: The Diva

In the city of Los Angeles, amidst the swaying palm trees, shining blue sky, and famous boulevards, Barbie was the symbolic "daughter" of the American movie culture known as "Dreamland." "Hollywood Boulevard is the heart of the heartless Hollywood legend. . . . You came here to find the wish fulfilled in 3-D among the flowers; the evasive child-world projected insistently into adulthood . . . the make-believe among the awesome palm trees that the invitation of technicolored gold-laced Movies . . . have promised is long distance for oh so long." John Rechy used these words in *City of Night* to describe this land of promises. Who better than a "heartless" girl to represent the cruel and glittering city, one that has always been a tireless factory of models and actresses suspended between reality and illusion? Barbie, who has no heart and no emotions, was the ideal actress waiting for her director. If, absurdly, she were made into a real woman, Barbie could live well between Sunset and Hollywood boulevards, close to the legendary hills covered with whitewashed villas, home to earthbound gods. No one would ever be the wiser.

It is true that Barbie's star quality is never obscured, not even when she is dressed in the simplest apparel and working in a traditional career. Her true identity is always that of the quintessential actress, for whom there are no primary or secondary roles because her existential motivation is to interpret all of them with equal passion. Her very wardrobe is worthy of a diva, complete with sumptuous and spectacular pieces that fit beautifully in the realm of high society. In the hands of children Barbie becomes a passive interpreter of the characters that they want to create; just like a puppet she recites the script and adapts to the rules of their game.

NEW!

#0490

Barbie® & Ken®
LITTLE THEATRE

The perfect place to star Barbie and Ken in your own plays! You'll have exciting, dramatic fun with this sturdy, easy-to-assemble theatre. Realistic stage with cloth curtain that can be raised and lowered. Theatrical backdrops, scenery and props; book of 7 original plays; special tickets for each play. Folds into handy carrying case, simple to store when not in use. (Dolls and costumes not included) $8.00

The Theater

There is no shortage of starting points. Mattel has specified various themes, taking them from the most popular repertory of theater and fables, and including even the grandest movie productions. All of this is intended to make the evolution of her image ever more dazzling by including her in those glamourous roles. "Barbie & Ken Little Theatre" (#4090) came out in 1964, and was a real theater complete with different sets. It is uncertain who the designer was, but we know that Gordon Shiremann, the draftsman of earlier Barbie environments (house, atelier, etc.) was involved in the project. Like these other structures, the theater was fabricated in cardboard that folded into a kind of carrying case. Once assembled, it became a proper theater with nineteenth-century influences, complete with a ticket office, cash register, posters, program, and a 96-page libretto with the texts of seven different plays. The brightly colored sets, which opened onto the stage with an ornate proscenium flanked by two box seats, were rendered realistically and were designed for plays that always starred Ken and Barbie. There were sets for "Cinderella" and "Little Red Riding Hood," as well as one with an Oriental theme and another inspired by the Knights of the Round Table. It sold for eight dollars. Obviously, the stars had the relevant costumes—purchased separately—at their disposal so they could dress up as the

*Facing page: The
advertisement for
"Barbie & Ken Little
Theatre" (1964), from
a catalog of that year.*

*Left: Barbie wears
"Guinevere" (1964–
65) and Ken is
dramatic in
"King Arthur"
(1964–65).*

123
....

appropriate characters. The "Cinderella" (#0872) ensemble was designed by Aileen Zublin, Kay Carter, and Dorothy Schue, and contained two outfits: one dress of plain sackcloth, and the fabulous enchanted dress for the ball. The "Prince" (#0772) borrowed from Renaissance designs for a Ken in tights and green velvet. Inspired by *The Thousand and One Nights*, there was "Barbie Arabian Night" (#0874), a splendid pink sari decorated with printed gold motifs resembling Aladdin's lamp, and, for Ken, "Arabian Night" (#0774), an outfit of red velvet jacket, tight pants of gold lamé, and the obligatory turban.

Bob Mackie, a fashion stylist for the stars of Hollywood, designed an auspicious series of Barbie dolls with meticulous care and attention to detail to be released in limited editions explicitly for the adult public of collectors. On the facing page,

"Neptune Fantasy" (1992), with the original sketch; above, "Madame du Barbie" (1997), and right, "Moon Goddess" (1996).

*On this page are two film stills from **Gone With the Wind** (1939), in which the actress Vivien Leigh, in the role of the heroine, Scarlett O'Hara, wears some of the character's most celebrated dresses, recreated for Barbie in 1994 and 1995 (facing page).*

The conspiracies at the court of King Arthur were staged in costumes for "Guinevere" (#0873), a severe and sumptuous dress in blue velvet, and "King Arthur" (#0773), a king in knight's garb armed with a scabbard, shield, and the infamous sword "Excalibur."

In Mattel's Autumn 1964 sales catalog, a gift package was advertised with the serial number 1018. Selling for twenty-five dollars, it contained all of these theatrical costumes, which sold individually for 3 or 4 dollars, along with the Ken and Barbie dolls. This gift pack was also promoted on television, increasing its sales success.

This theater episode and Barbie's related involvement with the world of entertainment remained isolated items within Mattel's vast market of products in the 1960s

and '70s. Not until 1989 would the promotional zeal inspired by the film world resume. The Barbie doll collecting phenomenon was growing substantially during these years and had begun to attract an adult audience. Mattel now turned to this emerging market and proposed special series of dolls dressed in extremely popular images of the collective imagination. Bob Mackie, a well-known stylist to the Hollywood stars, was invited by Mattel in 1989 to design a new line of fabulously dressed dolls in limited editions. This complex operation commanded all of the firm's creative forces in a painstaking collaboration whose goal was to achieve a product as close as possible to the intentions of its creator. And price was no object. Initially there were problems in the manufacture of the prototypes; they were not adequately successful when compared to the project's original sketch. Numerous adjustments were made with Bob Mackie working hands-on alongside Mattel's creative staff. Finally, in 1990, the first successful prototype in the new collector's series, the "Golden Mackie Barbie," was released. The doll was conceived and executed

The 1939 movie **The Wizard of Oz** inspired these costumes for Barbie—as Dorothy (1995) and Glinda The Good Witch (1996)—and Ken as the Tin Man (1996). On the lower left, a scene from the film with the main characters and the heroine, Dorothy, played by Judy Garland.

with the designer's utmost care, even down to the hairdo and makeup, with the collaboration of Stephen Tarmichael from the hair-styling division, and Hiroe Okubo-Wolf, who mastered the special facial makeup. This doll led to the production of what would become, thanks to annual editions, one of the most sought-after and collected series in the world. In the years to come, "Platinum Barbie" and "Starlight Barbie" (1991) were followed by the spectacular "Empress Bride" and "Neptune Fantasy" (1992), "Masquerade Ball" (1993), "Queen of Hearts" (1994), "Goddess of the Sun" (1995), and "Moon Goddess" (1996). The richness of the costumes, the elaborate hairdos, the jewels, even the very names of the dolls send the eyes and the memory back to the shimmering world of Busby Berkeley's musicals and the great American revue, in which

My Fair Lady, one of the most famous film musicals of the 1960s, starring Audrey Hepburn in the role of Eliza Doolittle, was refashioned by Barbie in 1996. Below, the original playbill.

Star Trek has become a global legend in the medium of science-fiction television and cinema. On the occasion of its 30th anniversary in 1996, Barbie and Ken reinvented its famous characters.

130

an ensemble of stupendous dancers was unfurled in perfect choreography. The statuesque creatures covered with lamé and shining sequins in the *Ziegfeld Follies*, who symbolized modern goddesses suspended between classical reminiscence and pagan fantasy, thus found a new incarnation in this series of dolls who perfectly evoked their splendor.

The Movies

A film of colossal proportions, the 1939 movie *Gone With the Wind* is a timeless legend of great American cinema, a stirring tale of the perseverance of will triumphing over adversity. Taken from the novel by Margaret Mitchell, it was adapted to the screen with a mid-nineteenth-century Southern ambiance that was accurately reconstructed with highly detailed historical criteria. It immediately became one of the major commercial successes of Hollywood. Michael Wood wrote about it in his book *America in the*

Movies: "A lot of films and a lot of money were made during the thirties too, of course, but it was not really until the time of *Gone With the Wind* that Hollywood perfected that broad and knowing flamboyance which became its trademark." And of course it was the film's memorable heroine Scarlett O'Hara, played by Vivien Leigh, whom Barbie recreated when Mattel put the "Hollywood Legends" series into production in 1994. The screen character who answered with hope the cruelest misfortune and destruction of everyday life, who sent the world her sagacious message with the famous line, "I'll think about it tomorrow. Tomorrow is another day," became a model of proud independence that was sublimely female. However, it wasn't very credible when observed in the context of O'Hara's own times. If her attitudes and actions were laughable for their obstinacy and hopeful faith, the fabulous dresses she wore yet became, in the midst of such tragedy, the true stars of this production.

Another timeless legend is Marilyn Monroe, with whom Barbie should fear no comparison, so huge is her own popularity. In this version from 1997, she evokes one of the most famous images of the actress, taken from the widely known sequence of the 1955 movie, **The Seven-Year Itch.**

Who better than Barbie, then, to wear these costumes? No other doll could afford the comparison with this grandiose image. The most improbable dress that the ingenious Scarlett wore was surely the one in green velvet with gold fringe and tassels, created with sartorial mastery out of the rich, heavy curtains that hung in Tara, Scarlett's

This page: Barbie wearing another famous costume of Marilyn Monroe's from the 1953 film **Gentlemen Prefer Blondes.**

family plantation that managed to survive the Civil War. Faithful to the "tapestry" aesthetic (so-called for the abundance of ornaments like bows, tassels, pom-poms, lace trimmings, and borders that had a certain success in fashion around the 1870s), this design showed itself for exactly what it was, a pretentious assemblage that would not fool the astute Rhett Butler. The identical design re-created by Mattel for Barbie opened this new series, meticulously respecting the features of the original. Also produced in 1994 was the Ken doll in Rhett's elegant attire—black tails—and the Clark Gable mustache. Another outfit chosen from the film, to the delight of collectors and movie fans everywhere, was the scandalous red dress in which Scarlett attended Melanie's birthday party, an outcast still exquisite in her depravity. The version created for Barbie, with her hair appropriately tied up at the nape of her neck in tiny chestnut-colored ringlets, was faithful to the crimson-red velvet original, with a full cape of matching tulle bordered in marabou. The dramatically draped design was simplified but remained strongly evocative of that flaming-red vision. In 1995 Barbie emerged in a replica of the film's most famous ensemble, a luminous green-and-white hoop skirt with a wide-brimmed straw hat and a matching parasol, worn by Scarlett during the picnic at the Twelve Oaks estate at the beginning of the movie. The last outfit to emerge from the series that year was the black-and-white dress worn by a married Scarlett in yet another of her attempts to seduce the steadfast Rhett Butler.

The display cartons for the various dolls in this series were printed with photographs from the original film and included a miniature poster of the movie.

The interpretations of legendary stories and films was not limited to *Gone with the Wind*. In 1995 Barbie wore the costume of Dorothy, heroine of *The Wizard of Oz*, copying the actress Judy Garland right down to her magic red slippers. In 1996 she appeared in the guise of Glinda The Good Witch, and an enormously successful version of Ken in the role of the Tin Man kept her company. These three characters faithfully represented the costumes from the legendary 1939 musical whose melodies, in the voice of Judy Garland, have become famous all over the world.

Among the major cinematographic successes of the 1960s, *My Fair Lady*, starring the graceful, beautiful actress Audrey Hepburn, was the happy result of transposing a famous stage musical to the big screen. This comedy was a modern version of the tale of Pygmalion, taking the characters to a more contemporary setting in London of the Belle Epoque. Some of the rich costumes created for this movie, from styles in fashion during the first decade of the century, were reproduced in miniature for Barbie in the context of the "Hollywood Legends" series. Marketed in 1996, we find Barbie dressed up as the poor and ignorant flower vendor, Eliza Doolittle, before her encounter with Professor Higgins, impersonated by Ken, who would transform her into a distinguished, fascinating lady. The designs that Mattel took from the movie were the most sumptuous—worn by the heroine to Ascot, to the ambassador's ball, and in the final scene of the film. Among the enormous hats with ostrich feathers and the tight-fitting dresses with trains, our Barbie once again seemed perfectly comfortable in this role. The commercial success that made Barbie the world's heroine was always well calibrated, emphasizing as always the versatility of this doll. She consistently manages to give shape to her past influences, with whom even many great contemporary actors would happily avoid comparing themselves.

133

Facing page: Barbie as Marilyn wearing the pink dress from the movie's performance of "Diamond;" above, the red dress worn for the celebrated song from the opening sequence in which Marilyn is coupled with the provocative brunette Jane Russell, who performs in an identical flashing sequined dress.

Barbie

and the Colors of the World

A Cross-Cultural Journey

The first Barbie with dark skin to appear on the international market was in 1980. The doll is shown on these pages wearing her debut dress.

Bring me the fairest creature northward born,

Where Phoebus' fire scarce thaws the icicles,

And let us make incision for your love,

To prove whose blood is reddest, his or mine.

(William Shakespeare, *The Merchant of Venice*)

Our Western system of development, a civilization defined by freedom of choice, instinctively fosters what it recognizes within its own parlance. Anything of an ethnically and/or culturally different matrix is measured with another yardstick in terms of value. For centuries, the evolution of human society occurred within circumscribed geographic locations, where traditions and attitudes assumed distinct characteristics and identities. Certain historic events—war, journey and expedition, and discovery—established a contact among diverse social groups that was not always beneficial to the growth of the two parties. More often than not, it brought about disastrous human tragedies and the subjugation of cultures that ended with the total destruction of great civilizations.

Today, in a time when few geographic boundaries are uncrossed and no distance seems too great to travel, the cross-cultural mix of ethnicities has become a modern-day reality. Many diverse races come together, sharing religions and traditions, moving human society closer to a more peaceful means of coexistence.

Collecting Ethnic Dolls

In every culture, certain rooted customs and ancient traditions persist, bound to the group's individuality. Among these, the amusement of playtime and toys often constitute a substructure, particularly dolls, who find themselves at the center of human progress across time and history as constant, vigilant witnesses and precious historical documents of a bygone way of life. In observing dolls from different societies, we are struck above all by the enormous variety of physical models representing man, as well as by the chromatic differences—the strong and contrasting colors—that makes these objects recognizable. The ultimate significance of these dolls within play and ritual is often hard ·to decipher, especially by those unfamiliar with a certain culture. But the fascination with their clothing and the evocative power of form and color in tribal ornaments, can nonetheless charm the most sophisticated western observer. These superficial aspects were probably the most attractive in inspiring travelers to start collecting dolls during their first voyages of conquest and discovery. The contemporary nuclei of great doll collections—tribal figures and fetishes—are displayed in ethnographic museums all over the world. Today, these collections are important for understanding the dolls' uses and fashions in cultural groups that have partially disappeared or have at least lost some of their ancient traditions. These were the model for the dolls in traditional costumes that became popular in the twentieth century, launching a widespread consumer market of travel souvenirs. Thus, these highly colorful little dolls of celluloid, polystyrene, and plastic, packaged in transparent boxes, become the favorite gift item with which to recall a pleasant sojourn abroad or to begin a collection.

The first series that dressed Barbie and Ken in the traditional costumes of various countries indicated a renewed corporate interest in this market. "Barbie & Ken Doll's Travel Costumes" involved exotic clothing for a dream vacation's ideal itinerary through the most evocative lands of every typical American's imagination. Produced in 1964, these costumes were always conceived in male/female pairs, except for the red

The 1985 version of Japanese Barbie. The features are carefully modeled on Asian traits. The sketch below shows the preceding "Barbie in Japan" from 1964.

Facing page: A dreamy destination for Barbie's world travels.

#0821

A MATTEL® TRAVEL COSTUME
BARBIE® IN JAPAN
Gorgeous costume includes red and gold brocade kimono; white and gold obi (sash); silver and red zōri (sandals) with white tabi; 3 kanzashis (hair ornaments); ōgi (fan), and a samisen (3-stringed banjo-like Japanese instrument). Story included. (without doll) $3.50

Below: Dutch Barbie (1994). Blond braids, starched cap, long striped skirt, and the inevitable clogs constitute the elements of one of the most popular folkloric costumes.

Above: Mexican Barbie (1996). Bright colors on a cotton print dress and black hair styled in a traditional braid are unmistakable stereotypes used to imply an authentic atmosphere.

The Hawaiian islands now belong to the popular imagination as a land of dreams and eternal spring—an ideal destination for vacations, as is often depicted in literature and film.

This "Polynesian Barbie" (1995) is a lively interpretation of Hawaii's exotic costume.

Long black hair, a headdress and lei of tropical flowers, and a grass skirt for dancing the hula are the familiar components of this

139

basic and lovely costume, a complement to the islands' culture and climate. This doll is the slightly modified

second edition of an earlier "Hawaiian Barbie" that appeared in 1975.

Japanese kimono (#0821), which was printed with gold and richly accessorized exclusively for Barbie. Other stopovers on this make-believe journey included Mexico, Switzerland, Holland, and the lush islands of Hawaii, each represented by traditional costume. Packaged with the dress and its accessories was a little travel book printed in color with a brief narrative, and the price for each ensemble varied between $1.50 and $3.50.

A Doll in Every Color

The dolls in this series were sold individually until 1980, when Mattel marketed a collector's set, "The Dolls of the World Collection," that now includes more than forty different subjects. In it, the most striking element was

Above: "Parisian Barbie" (1997). This is a second version of a similar doll that came out in 1980.

Right: "Ghanaian Barbie" (1996) wears a dress printed with bright tribal motifs and has a perfect ethnic characterization.

principally chromatic, with a range of strong and contrasting colors that characterized the fabrics and accessories of the lovely ethnic outfits.

Away from the world of fashion and the spectacle of the movies momentarily, Barbie was now being used to represent different races and cultures all over the globe, carefully interpreting the world's national costumes.

This series continues to grow and spread quite successfully, perpetuating an ancient tradition of collecting dolls in folkloric costumes. For its part, Mattel has been careful to concentrate maximum effort on the sartorial aspects, attempting to give every doll the spirit of an immediately recognizable national and geographic origin. To that end, they have not always borrowed Barbie's standard physiognomy, as her facial features would too often differ from those to be portrayed. Mattel was sensitive to this requirement, choosing various prototypes for the face and changing the makeup, the skin color, the eyes, and the hair accordingly, mindful of what would be most appropriate for a particular folk costume.

Many Barbies for Many Girls

We ought to clarify that in Ruth Handler's original concept, Barbie was to serve above all as a mirror image onto which the child at play could transfer and then compare her fantasies with other realities. Following this principle, Mrs. Handler was quickly aware that the international market to which Barbie was, and is, addressed could not be identified with just one set of features or race. It was a problem that emerged with greater clarity in the 1970s, with the conquest of market sectors in many different countries.

For a child the doll must therefore guarantee a sense of security in the face of an uncertain universe, one

Indian Barbie from 1996 follows an earlier version from 1982. In this recent edition, the doll is dressed in a richly traditional sari, complemented by customary jewelry and a caste mark on her forehead.

A Cross-Cultural Journey

Top left: "Arctic Barbie" from 1997 is the newer version of "Eskimo Barbie" from 1982.

Above right: "Puerto Rican Barbie" from 1997. Left: "Chinese Barbie" from 1994.

Facing page: "Russian Barbie" from 1997, in a new version of her 1989 predecessor. These four very different dolls represent races and costumes from all corners of the globe.

that she cannot test firsthand. This happens in a greater measure when our subject, the Barbie doll, represents a grownup, which is when it becomes even more important that she be easily recognizable.

This concept, which was destined to raise Barbie's level of distribution around the world, unites a multi-cultural commercial market with an easily adaptable product. For the first time in the history of doll making, the Barbie doll did not lose her real identity even though she was modified considerably to suit diverse ethnic expectations. The first example of a doll with nonconforming features was the creation of Christie in 1968. She was followed in 1969 by Julia, inspired by the actress Diahann Carroll, a popular television character of that time, and was designed with the same head prototype used in previous dolls. There were now two dolls with more realistic, typically African-American facial features.

On the male side we saw Brad in 1970 and Curtis in 1975, both of them black with well-defined features, while the dark-skinned Black Barbie made her debut on the international market in 1980, satisfying a huge portion of her clientele and marking the beginning of a new era in doll making. Other characters in Barbie's family changed the color of their skin over the years, just as numerous new friends from various nations arrived to further animate this increasingly international clan.

Mattel and its creative department began to turn their attention more to pinpointing the features needed to personalize the doll for its destined market. Thus we saw Hispanic Barbie in 1979 and Italian Barbie in 1980, whose facial features were stereotypically ethnic. African-American models Shani and her boyfriend Jamal, from 1991, were designed by Kitty Black Perkins and pro-duced to the highest standards of beauty and quality by the creative division at Mattel. These black dolls were a welcome addition to the Barbie family for the African-American cus-tomer, an essential part of the United States market.

143

The Japanese Problem

Among the many dolls manufactured for export, those destined for Japan required a special effort on Mattel's part. It seems incredible that Barbie would have the hardest time penetrating and finding popular success in this country, the birthplace of her production. The journalist Dara Kotnik addressed this issue when she wrote: "With oriental courtesy, the editor of a magazine specializing in the toy market said, 'It's the fault of the too-beautiful doll.'

This explains rather diplomatically why Mattel, the biggest toy producer in the world, has not been able to position itself among the twenty major toy suppliers in Japan. The fact is that Barbie has a smiling expression and little Japanese girls, who are used to covering their mouths when they laugh, are almost afraid of her. And the eyes? They are wide open and her expression is confident, almost arrogant. The clothes? They are conspicuous, the expression of an independent life, of easy money, and of tastes that are questionable but are certainly expensive."

Mattel responded quickly to these observations and adapted Barbie's look to incorporate feedback from the Japanese market. The new Barbie was transformed from the one universally known: the expression was mild, the lips were only slightly parted in a smile, the eyes were brown, the skin was pale, the "scandalous" bust was less buxom, and the legs were long but the feet were shaped for flat shoes. Even the hair, though it was still blond in response to the popularity of dyed hair among Japanese teenagers, was pulled back in a simple ponytail, rejecting the vivacious western-style tresses. In place of the usual repertory of coordinated accessories, these ensembles came with items symbolic of the domesticated woman: pots and pans; baby bottles and little carriages for baby dolls; shopping bags; tender little stuffed animals; and dresses that expressed the prudence of a good housewife rather than fashion-conscious vanity.

It should be noted that another concept of Barbie that is very different from the one currently in distribution does exist in Asia.

144

Above: "English Barbie" (1992), inspired by Mary Poppins. Right: "Malaysian Barbie" (1991), has a face with highly characteristic Asian features. The gilded fabrics in bright colors give the costume an added touch of exoticism.

In 1982, a Japanese toy factory, Takara, produced dolls under license from Mattel exclusively for the Asian market. In 1986, the license passed to another local factory called Ma-Ba, an acronym of it parent company names Mattel and Bandai.

Though the Barbie logo was identical on the doll packaging, as were the names of the various characters in her world, the image of the product was profoundly different from her American "parent." With her wide, plumper face, rounded eyes, and shoulder-length blond hair with bangs, this doll resembled the animated cartoons then popular in Japan.

Right:
"Jamaican Barbie" (1992).
Below left:
"Barbie Italiana" (1993), with the imposing Colosseum as a backdrop.
Below right:
"German Barbie" (1995).

If further proof were necessary at this point, then this is the ultimate confirmation that endless research was compiled over the many years that went into changing the Barbie doll's image from the single, repetitive original model into a personalized subject for children of all cultures; Barbie was the essence of a truly international toy.

Her adaptability, her ongoing ability to be a precise point of reference for the juvenile imagination and—why not, at this point?—the adult one, too, broke down geographic, political, and racial barriers, all

The 1968 Christie doll met with considerable fame and success on a par with the subsequent Julia doll. In the talking edition, she can express herself in English, French, German, and Spanish. Here Christie wears the "Ruffles 'N Swirls" outfit (1970). This beautiful doll has the "Twist 'N Turn" body with a waist that turns and legs that bend at the knee.

The dolls in the "World Collection"*

1980	Italian Barbie, Parisian Barbie, Royal Barbie (England)
1981	Scottish Barbie, Oriental Barbie
1982	Eskimo Barbie, East India Barbie
1983	Spanish Barbie, Swedish Barbie
1984	Irish Barbie, Swiss Barbie
1985	Japanese Barbie
1986	Greek Barbie, Peruvian Barbie
1987	German Barbie, Icelandic Barbie
1988	Korean Barbie, Canadian Barbie
1989	Russian Barbie, Mexican Barbie
1990	Nigerian Barbie, Brazilian Barbie
1991	Malaysian Barbie, Czechoslovakian Barbie
1992	Jamaican Barbie
1993	Native American Barbie, Australian Barbie
1994	Dutch Barbie, Chinese Barbie, Kenyan Barbie
1995	Polynesian Barbie, German Barbie, Irish Barbie
1996	Japanese Barbie, Indian Barbie, Mexican Barbie, Norwegian Barbie, Ghanaian Barbie
1997	French Barbie, Russian Barbie, Arctic Barbie, Puerto Rican Barbie

* Listed by the name used for international distribution.

Left: Shani (1991) wears the "Purple Dress" design by Kitty Black Perkins; she represents a successful outcome of the experimentation with exotic physiognomies.

Right: Hispanic Barbie (1989).

with a single objective and unifying desire as old as mankind—to indulge the imagination, the magic of make-believe, the inevitable urge in all of us to play.

In 1997 "Rapunzel" was introduced to the American market, after the famous fairy-tale character. Impersonating the young princess with her celebrated long braids, Barbie debuted a different face conceived by Mattel's creative staff. The new features derived from a careful analysis of teenage aesthetic and behavioral trends and are based on a completely new facial casting that is enhanced with light makeup to achieve a fresher, more youthful and natural look.

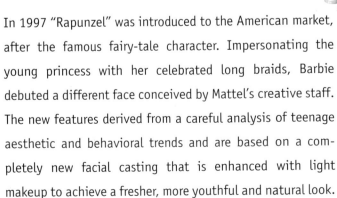

Facing page: African-American and Caucasian Barbie dolls with various shades of hair in the "Cool Blue" series—representative of the doll's latest aesthetic evolution.

Below: Barbie in the "Bead Blast" series, furnished with beads for both the doll's hair and that of her new owner. A fresh new image characterizes Barbie on the eve of the year 2000.

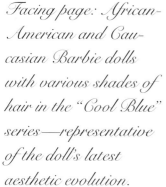

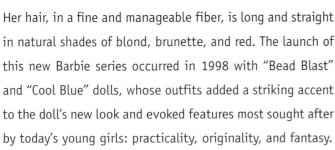

Her hair, in a fine and manageable fiber, is long and straight in natural shades of blond, brunette, and red. The launch of this new Barbie series occurred in 1998 with "Bead Blast" and "Cool Blue" dolls, whose outfits added a striking accent to the doll's new look and evoked features most sought after by today's young girls: practicality, originality, and fantasy.

Still to come is a model called "Really Rad" Barbie, which will debut a doll with a more teen-like physique.

Selected Bibliography

Ashabraner, Joan, and Sibyl De Wein. *The Collector's Encyclopedia of Barbie Dolls and Collectibles*. Paducah, Ky: Collector Books, 1977.

Aspesi, N., et al., *Alta Moda. Grandi abiti da sera degli anni '50/'60 (Haute Couture: Great Evening Gowns of the Fifties and Sixties)*. Exhibition catalogue, Venice: n.p., 1984.

Blitman, Joe. *Francie & Her Mod, Mod, Mod, Mod World of Fashions*. Grantsville, Md: Hobby House Press, 1996.

———. *Vive la Francie, An Illustrated Guide to Francie's Wardrobe*. Los Angeles: Joe Blitman, 1992.

Boy, Billy. *Barbie: Her Life & Times and the New Theater of Fashion*. New York: Crown Publishers, 1992.

Caillois, Roger. *I giochi e gli uomini (Man, play, and games)*. Milan: n.p., 1981.

Coleman, Dorothy S., Elisabeth A. Coleman, and Evelin J. Coleman. *Collector's Book of Doll's Clothes*. New York: n.p., 1976.

Deutsch, Stefanie. *Barbie the First 30 Years: 1959 Through 1989*. Paducah, Ky: Collector Books, 1996.

Devlin, Polly. *Vogue 1920–1980. Moda, Immagine, Costume (Vogue Book of Fashion Photography: 1919–1979)*. Milan: n.p., 1980.

Eames, Sarah Sink. *Barbie Fashion, Volume I: 1959–1967*. Paducah, Ky: Collector Books, 1990.

Farago, Stephanie, et al., *The Magic and Romance of Art Dolls*. Los Angeles: Farago Publishers, 1986.

Fennick, Janine. *The Collectible Barbie Doll: An Illustrated Guide to Her Dreamy World*. Philadelphia: Running Press, Courage Books, 1996.

Fox, Carl. *The Doll*. New York: Harry N. Abrams, 1973.

Handler, Ruth, with Jacqueline Shannon. *Dream Doll: The Ruth Handler Story*. Stamford, Ct: Longmeadow Press, 1994.

Hellman, Walter. *Barbie. Kunstler und Designer gestalten für und um Barbie (Barbie: Artist and Designer Fashions for and about Barbie)*. Exhibition catalogue, Hamburg: n.p., 1994.

Jacobs, Laura. *Barbie: What a Doll!*. New York: Abbeville, 1994.

Lord, M. G. *Forever Barbie: The Unauthorized Biography of a Real Doll*. New York: Avon Books, 1994.

Mandeville, A. Glenn. *Doll Fashion Anthology and Price Guide*. Grantsville, Md: Hobby House Press, 1996.

Manos, Paris and Susan Manos. *The World of Barbie Dolls*. Paducah, Ky: Collector Books, 1983.

Palli, Fulvia Gicca. *La bambola (The Doll)*. Florence: n.p., 1990.

Pisetzky, Rosita Levi. *Il costume e la moda nella società italiana (Dress and Fashion in Italian Society)*. Turin: n.p., 1978.

Sacchi, Antonio, and Davide Turconi, eds., *Divi & Divine (Divas and Goddesses)*. Exhibition catalogue, Florence: Casa Usher, 1981.

Silvestrini, E. and E. Simeoni, eds., "La cultura della bambola," *La Rivista Folklorica* 16 (1987).

Shibano, Keiko Kimura. *Barbie in Japan*. Kenosha, Wi: n.p., 1994.

Steele, Valerie. *Art, Design & Barbie: The Evolution of a Cultural Icon*. Exhibition catalogue, New York: Exhibitions International, 1995.

Tarnowska, Maree. *Poupées de Mode (Fashion Dolls)*. Paris: n.p., 1986.

Theimer, François. *Barbie: poupée de collection (Barbie: A Collectible Doll)*. Paris: n.p., 1985.

Tosa, Marco. *Bambole (Dolls)*. Milan: Idealibri S.p.A., 1993.

———. *Bambole Lenci (Lenci Dolls)*. Milan: Idealibri S.p.A., 1989.

———. *Classic Dolls*. New York: Abbeville, 1989

———. *Effetto bambola (The Doll Effect)*. Milan: Idealibri S.p.A., 1988.

———. *Evening Dresses: 1900–1940*. New York: Quite Specific Media Group Ltd., Drama Publishers, 1997.

———. *Le Bambole (The Doll)*. Milan: Idealibri S.p.A., 1990.

Westenhouser, Kitturah B. *The Story of Barbie*. Paducah, Ky: Collector Books, 1994.

Wood, Michael. *America in the Movies, or "Santa Maria, It Had Slipped My Mind"*. New York: Basic Books, 1975.

Index of Models

Numbers in italic refer to the illustrations. Numbers in bold refer to the dolls pictured in the gatefold (pages 37–44).

BARBIE AND KEN MODELS

All Decked Out (1997): **6**, **24**
Amethyst, Bob Mackie Jewel Series (1997): **19**
Barbie American Girl (1965): *33*, 36
Barbie Bubble Cut (1961): *22*, *27*, 34
Barbie Fashion Queen (1963): *29*, 35, 36, *81*
Barbie for President (1992): *121*
Barbie Loves Elvis Giftset (1997): **28**
Barbie Number One (1959): *18*, *19*, *21*, *26*, 32–34
Barbie Number Two (1959): 34
Barbie Number Three (1960): 34
Barbie Number Four (1960): 34
Barbie Superstar (1997): *44*, 45
Barbie Swirl Ponytail (1963–64): *29*, 36
Barbie Twist 'N Turn (1967): *34*, 37, *146*
Bead & Blast (1998): 149, *149*
Benefit Ball Barbie (1992): *106*, 111
Billions of Dreams (1997): *109*
Black Barbie (1980): *134*, *135*, 143
Blue Rhapsody (1986): 110
Chinese Empress, Great Eras Series (1997): **25**
City Slickers (1997): **10**, **15**
"Classique" Series: *106*
Color Magic Barbie (1966): 37
Cool Colors (1998): *148*, 149
Court Favorite (1997): **11**
"Designer" Series: *110*, 111, *111*
Diamond, Bob Mackie Jewel Series (1997): **1**, **27**
Doctor Barbie (1994): *120*
Emerald, Bob Mackie Jewel Series (1997): **17**
Empress Bride, Bob Mackie Barbie (1992): 129, **13**
Fashion Jeans Barbie (1982): *105*
French Lady, Great Eras Series (1997): **5**, **18**
Goddess of the Sun (1994): 129
Gold, Bob Mackie Jewel Series (1991): **9**, **30**
Golden Mackie Barbie (1990): 126
Ken (1961): *28*, 35, 36, *67*, *68*, *72*, *73*, 74, 88, *123*, 125, *126*, *128*, *130*, *132*, *133*, 136
Live Action Barbie (1971): *103*, 107
Madame du Barbie (1997): *125*
Masquerade Ball (1993): 129
Midnight Gala (1995): **3**, **16**
Midnight Princess (1997): **26**

Miss Barbie (1964): *31*, 36
Moon Goddess (1996): *125*, 129
Neptune Fantasy Barbie (1992): *124*, 129
Patriot, American Stories Series (1997): **14**, **29**
Perfectly Suited Giftset (1997): **12**
Platinum Barbie (1991): 129
Queen of Hearts (1994): 129
Rapunzel (1997): 148
Romantic Interlude (1997): **23**
Sissi (1996): *112*
Starlight Barbie (1991): 129
Starlight Waltz Barbie (1995): **2**, **21**
Sugar Plum Fairy (1997): **8**, **22**
Talking Barbie (1968): 37
Talking Busy Barbie (1972): *35*
Talking Julia (1969): *36*, 143
Totally Hair Barbie (1992): *104*
Twiggy (1967): *102*, 104
Uptown Chic Barbie (1994): **7**
Water Lili (1997): **4**

FRIENDS AND FAMILY

Allan (1964): *32*, 36, *67*, *68*, 74, *116*
Brad (1970): 143
Casey (1967): *96*, 104
Christie (1968): *44*, 143, *146*
Curtis (1975): 143
Francie (1966): 37, *96*, *97*, *101*, 102, 104
Jamal (1991): 143
Midge (1963): *28*, 35, 36, *67*, *68*, 74, 81
Ricky (1965): 36
Shani (1991): 143, *147*
Skipper (1964): *31*, 36, 74
Skooter (1965): 36
Stacey (1968): *96*

CLOTHING

1600 Series: *37*
After Five (1962–64): *91*
All That Jazz (1968): *96*
American Airlines Stewardess (1961–64): 116, *117*
Astro Fashion Collection (1985): 108
Ballerina (1961–65): 118, *118*
Barbie Baby-Sits (1963–64): 118
Barbie in Japan (1964): *137*, 140
Barbie-Q Outfit (1959–62): *70*, 71, *71*
Benefit Performance (1966–67): *93*
Black Magic Ensemble (1964–65): 81, *81*

Business Appointment (1966–67): *88*
Busy Gal (1960–61): *80*
Busy Morning (1963): *55*
Campus Hero (1961–64): *68*
Campus Sweetheart (1965): *87*, 95
Career Girl (1963–64): *88*
Caribbean Cruise (1967): 102
Cheerleader (1964–65): *68*
Clear Out (1967): *96*
Color Coordinates (1964–65): *75*
Commuter Set (1959–60): *48*, *62*, 68
Cotton Casual (1959–62): 71, *76*, *77*
Culotte Wot (1968): *97*
Debutante Ball (1966–67): *81*
Denims On! (1967): *96*
Drum Majorette (1964–65): *68*
Easter Parade (1959): *49*, *60*, 63
Enchanted Evening (1960–63): *84*, *85*, 93
Evening Splendour (1959–64): *61*, 64
Fashion Luncheon (1966–67): *95*, 97
Fashion Shiner (1967–68): *95*
Fashion Undergarments (1959–62): *65*, 71
Floral Petticoat (1959–63): *65*, 71
Fountain Boy (1964–65): *75*
Friday Nite Date (1960–64): *52*, *53*
Gad-About (1966): *101*
Gay Parisienne (1959): *49*, *58*, 60
Gold 'N Glamour (1965): *97*
Holiday Dance (1965–66): 81
Jump into Lace (1968): *100*
Lemon Kick (1970): *99*
Lovely Lingerie pak (1964–67): *65*
Magnificence (1965): *94*
Matinee Fashion (1965): *93*
Me 'N My Doll (1964–66): *31*
Miss Astronaut (1965): 116, *116*
Modern Art (1965): *33*
Mr. Astronaut (1965): 116
Nighty-Negligee Set (1959–64): *65*, 71
On the Avenue (1965): *93*, 97
Open Road (1961–64): *79*
Orange Zip (1968): *96*
Patio Party (1967–68): 102
Peachy Fleecy Coat (1959–61): 71
Picnic Set (1959–61): *69*, 71
Plantation Belle (1959–61): *56*, *57*, 59
Print Aplenty (1967–68): *101*
Purple Dress (1991): *147*
Red Flare (1962–65): *86*, 95
Registered Nurse (1961–64): *115*, 118
Resort Set (1959–62): 71
Roman Holiday (1959): *49*, 59
Rovin Reporter (1965): *32*
Ruffles 'N Swirls (1970): *146*

Satin Bolero (1963): *92*
Saturday Matinee (1965): *89, 97*
Senior Prom (1963–64): *87, 91, 95*
Solo in the Spotlight (1960–64): *83, 92*
Sophisticated Lady (1963–64): *94*
Sorority Meeting (1962–63): *28*
Student Teacher (1965–66): 118, *119*
Suburban Shopper (1959–64): *48, 54, 57*
Sunflower (1967–68): *98,* 101
Sweater Girl (1959–62): *51,* 57
Sweet Dreams (1959–63): 71
Tennis Anyone? (1962–64): *67*
Theatre Date (1963): *92*
Time for Tennis (1962–63): *67*
Touchdown (1963–65): *68*
Tuxedo (1961–65): *28, 72*
Twiggy Gear (1968): *102*
Wedding Day Set (1959–62): *72, 72, 73*
Winter Holiday (1959–63): 71

**CLOTHING AND CHARACTERS
FROM FILM AND THEATER**

Barbie Arabian Night (1964–65): 125
Cinderella (1964–65): 125

Cinderella (1997): **20**
Dorothy (1995): *128, 133*
Eliza Doolittle (1996): *129,* 133
Glinda The Good Witch (1996): *128, 133*
Guinevere (1964–65): *123,* 126
"Hollywood Legends" Series: 130, 133
Ken Arabian Night (1964–65): 125
King Arthur (1964–65): *123,* 126
Marilyn Monroe (1997): *131, 132, 133*
Prince (1964–65): 125
Professor Higgins (1996): 133
Rhett Butler (1994–95): 132
Scarlett O'Hara (1994–95): *127,* 132
Star Trek (1996): *130*
The Tin Man (1966): *128,* 133

INTERNATIONAL DOLLS

Arctic Barbie (1997): *142*
"Barbie & Ken Dolls' Travel Costumes" Series
  (1964): 136
Chinese Barbie (1994): *142*
The Dolls of the World Collection: 140
Dutch Barbie (1994): *138*
English Barbie (1992): *144*

Eskimo Barbie (1982): *142*
German Barbie (1995): *145*
Ghanaian Barbie (1996): *140*
Hawaiian Barbie (1975): *139*
Hispanic Barbie (1979): 143
Indian Barbie (1982 and 1992): 141, *141*
Italian Barbie (1980 and 1993): *145*
Jamaican Barbie (1992): *145*
Japanese Barbie (1985): *136, 137,* 143
Malaysian Barbie (1991): *144*
Mexican Barbie (1996): *138*
Parisian Barbie (1980 and 1997): *140*
Polynesian Barbie (1995): *139*
Puerto Rican Barbie (1996): *142*
Russian Barbie (1989 and 1997): 142, *143*

MISCELLANEOUS

Barbie & Ken Little Theatre (1964):
  122, *122*
Barbie Fashion Shop (1963): *90–91*
The New Theatre of Fashion (1985): 110

Photograph Credits

Blumenfeld (Courtesy *Vogue*. Copyright © 1950, renewed 1978 by The Condé Nast Publications, Inc.): 26 left; CBS, Inc.: 129 bottom right; Consiglio, Marco: 136 top; Haertter: 82; Halsman, Philippe, Magnum/Contrasto: 85 top; Klein, William (Courtesy *Vogue*. Copyright © 1962, renewed 1990 by The Condé Nast Publications, Inc.): 99 top; Used with permission from Mattel, Inc.: back cover, 6, 7, 8, 9, 10–11, 12, 13, 14, 15, 16, 17, 21 bottom, 25 top right, 26 right, 28 left, 29 top, 35 bottom, 38, 39, 40, 41, 42, 43, 45, 46, 49, 52, 55, 57 top left, 60, 62 left, 66–67, 68, 70, 73 top, 76, 78, 79 left, 80 left, 81 top, 83 top left, 84, 86 left, 90–91, 92, 93 center, 95 left, 98, 103, 104, 105, 106, 107, 108–109, 110, 111, 112, 114, 115 left, 117 left, 120, 121, 124, 125, 127, 128 left, top right, center, 129 top right and bottom left, 130 left,

131 right, 132 top, 133, 134, 135, 138, 139, 140, 141, 142, 143, 144, 145, 148, 149; Mondadori Archives: 22 left, 23 top left and right, 36 right, 44, 47, 50, 56 left, 57 top right and bottom, 59 bottom, 64 (Grazia Neri), 83 top right, 86 center right, 87 bottom, 97 center (Mario De Biasi), 100 right, 102 right, 113; Motto, Gianfranco: 22 right, 65 top left, 74, 75; Paramount Pictures: 130 top right; Private collection: 1, 2, 3, 4, 5, 18, 19, 20, 21 top, 23 bottom, 24, 25 left, 27, 28 right, 29 bottom, 30, 31, 32, 33, 34, 35 top, 36 left, 37, 48, 51, 53, 54, 56 bottom, 58, 59 top, 61, 62 right, 65, 66 bottom, 69, 71, 72, 73 bottom, 74, 75, 77, 79 right, 80 top right, 81 bottom, 83 bottom right, 85 bottom, 86 top right, 87 top, 88, 89, 91 bottom, 93 left and right, 94, 95 right, 96–97, 99 bottom, 100 left, 101, 102 left, 115 top

right, 116, 117 right, 118, 119, 122, 123, 136 bottom, 137, 146, 147; Rosener, Ann (Courtesy *Life* magazine): 63; Tosatto, Alessandro (Ag. Contrasto): 18, 21 top, 24, 27, 28 right, 30, 31 right, 32, 33, 34, 35 top, 36 left, 48, 51 left and top right, 54 right, 58, 59 top, 61 right, 66 bottom, 69 left, 72, 80 top right, 87 top, 88 left and bottom right, 89, 94, 95 right, 96–97, 97 top and bottom, 99 bottom, 100 left, 101, 102 left, 116, 119 left and bottom right, 123 left, 136 bottom, 137 left, 146, 147; Turner Entertainment: 56 left, 126, 128 bottom left; Twentieth Century Fox: 131 bottom left, 132 bottom.

Every effort has been made to contact the copyright holders for the photographs in this book. Any omissions will be corrected in subsequent editions.